THROUGH MY EYES

THROUGH MY EYES

A Memoir

Siegfried Bader

FCP

Full Court Press
Englewood Cliffs, New Jersey

First Edition

Copyright © 2014 by Siegfried Bader

Published in the United States of America
by Full Court Press, 601 Palisade Avenue
Englewood Cliffs, NJ 07632
www.fullcourtpressnj.com

ISBN 978-1-938812-29-3
Library of Congress Control No. 2014932187

Editing and Book Design by Barry Sheinkopf
for Bookshapers (www.bookshapers.com)

Colophon by Liz Sedlack

DEDICATION

To my family and friends
who shared these experiences with me

Table of Contents

AN ADVENTURE

I T STARTED WITH A GOOD-BYE at the train station in Salzburg, Austria, on November 15, 1956, with my mother, two grandmothers, my sister and her husband, two uncles and aunts, and some cousins. It was a heartbreaking good-bye for my wife, my daughter, and me. My two grandmothers were in their mid-seventies and were crying, "We will never see you again!"

They were right. They did not live to see me again.

My family, and my father-in-law, traveled from Salzburg to Nuremberg, where my wife's sister had a house, the next day. All the relatives living there came to the train station to say good-bye, too, which was also emotional.

From there we had to travel by train for a couple of hours to reach the airport in Munich.

The next day, my then-twenty-year-old wife, my eight-month-old daughter Hannelore, and I at twenty-four immigrated to the United States with a group of other immigrants, some with small children, and some older people. There were eighty-nine of us in all, destined for different places. My family's was Jeffersonville, in Sullivan County,

New York.

In order to qualify for air travel, you had to be old or have children with you; otherwise, you had to take a six-week crossing by ship. We qualified because my wife was pregnant with our second daughter.

We landed at Idlewild Airport (now Kennedy), not as passengers but as cargo, because this made it cheaper for the sponsoring agency. The aircraft was a Flying Tiger four-engine cargo transport. Normally, engine noise in an airplane is low because the passenger cabin is padded. There's no padding in a cargo plane. When it took off with full throttle on the engine, it was so loud that, when I took a look at my baby daughter, her mouth was wide open, and I knew she was screaming, but I couldn't hear her. I could see a lot of open mouths on other people in the plane, too, but the only noise was the sound of those engines!

We had to land for a refueling in Paris and in the Azore Islands. The flight should have ended in eighteen hours (you know, with no jets at that time, air travel was much slower). But the plane encountered a storm, which was a lot of fun too, going up and down with a lot of wiggling. This made the plane run short of fuel, so we had to land again in northern Canada. Because of the storm, the layover in Canada lasted for six hours, and nobody was allowed to get off the plane, not even the stewardesses. Only the flight crew changed, and from there we had another eight hours in the air to New York City. We ran out of food and milk for the babies. The two stewardesses were so tired, they let everybody do for themselves.

Suddenly, smoke appeared in the cabin! There were two electric cookers for warming the milk for the babies, and one of them hadn't been turned off. The water had boiled over, and the cooker had shorted out and was smoking, which made everyone worried, but the stewardesses handled the problem.

So the whole flight was from Munich to New York took thirty-two hours, without a break for anybody on the plane. One old woman got very sick, and with no doctor there, only the poor stewardess could help her. I never found out what happened to her.

We landed at a commercial part of the New York airport. From there, we were all taken by bus to some building in New York City, where a woman instructed us how to get to the right destination, in German—which was the last time we heard instructions in German. Our bus took my wife, daughter, and me to the Short Line bus terminal in Manhattan for the ride to Liberty, New York. Then there was a bus that stopped at Jeffersonville, where my wife's uncle and aunt were living. They had emigrated two years earlier to be with some of their relatives.

From the start of that Short Line bus trip on, nobody explained anything to us in German; the driver only spoke English. The rest of the passengers were all from the city, going to Grossinger's, a big hotel and recreation station in Liberty for skiing in winter. When the bus crossed the

George Washington Bridge into New Jersey, I had no idea that we had left the city.

My understanding of English was very limited as well, and my wife did not speak it at all. She started to cry, and said, "*Ich will zurückgehen*" ("I want to go back home," a litany I heard many, many times for the next two years before she finally settled down).

I had no idea how far Liberty was, so after an hour, the kid in me start to ask, "Are we there yet?" But none of the grown-ups understood me. There was a woman in the next line of seats who was looking at my wife and me a lot. My daughter was quite unruly after awhile, and my wife had her work cut out for her in quieting the child. This woman made, and still makes, me feel she was an actress I'd seen in some movie.

The bus made several stops, and, every time it did, I was prepared to get off, because I thought we had reached Liberty, but the driver said no. I realized he was stopping just to let passengers get off to buy some refreshments and come back. These stops included the Tower of Pizza in New Jersey and the Red Apple Rest in New York. I could not get off, though, since I had no money to buy anything, although my daughter needed some milk and my wife and I could have eaten something, too. When I left Europe, I had been allowed to bring $32.00 per person, and no more, to the United States, so I had a grand total of $96.00 dollars—but it was packed away in a bag in the bus compartment.

At the Red Apple Rest, the woman got off too, and when she came back she handed my wife and me a hamburger, and a bottle of milk for my daughter. It was a gift we have never forgotten. By then, it was indisputable to me that she was an actress I had seen in the movies. She said, "I go to Liberty, too. You go off the bus when I go."

After that, whenever the bus stopped, she just shook her head. In Liberty, she got off the bus so fast, we never saw her again, but my wife and I have never forgotten her.

That was four hours after leaving New York, and there was the son-in-law of my wife's uncle waiting for us. It was another two hours in the car to Jeffersonville.

When we got there, I started working in a garage, repairing cars, until 1958, when I left to work at the Ford Assembly Plant in Mahwah, New Jersey, where I worked for twenty-four more years, until the plant closed. We bought a house in Mahwah 1961; we have been living there ever since—over fifty-two years.

If we had moved back to Europe as my wife would have liked, my daughter would be reading this story today to some other people in another town—that is, if it had ever been written at all. What will now follow this is, of course, another story.

And if you have perhaps been falling asleep through this recital, hello there—and please wake up!

AN AIRPLANE CRASH

IN THE 1940S TO THE 1970S, Spring Valley, in New York State, had a small airport. I took flying lessons there, in a Cessna airplane, in early 1962.

For you, I imagine my airplane crash will be the most amusing part of that whole period in my life. Don't worry—I will not burden you with pilot jargon or flight glossaries. All I want to tell you about is my moment of horror, when it all went wrong. It still feels to me as if it happened just today.

It was a sunny early morning, and I was sitting in the cockpit of the Cessna, ready for takeoff. I wanted to practice flying cross-country to a small airport about fifty miles away. After landing there, I was planning to return to Spring Valley.

I'd had my pre-takeoff inspection, the engine was warmed up, and I had finished taxiing onto the runway, ready for takeoff. Another glance over the guages, then full throttle, and the airplane started to roll. When the aircraft reached the right speed, I pulled back slightly on the yoke. The nose of the plane rose, and the runway dropped away as I lifted off.

Once the wheels were up, I turned the airplane out of

the flight patterns. I cut back on the engine RPMs. I had to make a right turn and then straighten out, heading into the right direction. The altimeter read fifteen hundred feet. I wanted to climb to three thousand before leveling off.

Looking out the window, I could see the city, roads, houses, some quite tall buildings ahead of me, and a lake to my right. "I must not forget to look at the altimeter," I reminded myself. "Almost three thousand—time to level off."

I cut the engine back some more until the tachometer showed eighteen hundred RPM. My speed was then around the hundred-knot mark. Good, three thousand feet high, some "trimming" until the airplane settled down to an even flight. . .there's not much to do at such times but enjoy the scenery, glance sometimes at the guages, and wait until you reach your destination.

Fifteen minutes into the flight, I suddenly hit really strong turbulence. It lasted only a second or two, but it shook me. Boy, was I lucky! I thought. It almost turned me over. When I looked out the window again, I saw black clouds not far off and directly in front of me. How did this get there so fast? I wondered. Blinking my eyes did not help: The clouds were real. I mumbled, "Maybe I should turn around?"

At that moment, the turbulence returned and threw me onto a roller coaster.

By then I was sure I had to head back, and I turned around. How dumb can you get? Sure, I had checked out the airplane before I left—but I'd neglected to ask for a weather report, and now I'd pay for it. The day had seemed so clear and sunny, though, I hadn't expected any of what was happening.

The clouds closed in on me, and I could not see where I was flying. No problem—I switched the navigation radio, telling myself, "It will guide me home."

Two minutes later, it went dead.

"Just don't panic! Get lower, out of the cloud!" I told myself. But this was easier said than done: The turbulence was terrible—shoving me up one moment and down the next. Between those elevator rides, the airplane bounced from side to side like a toy.

It suddenly came to my mind that, if an alien on a spaceship looked for my stomach just then, with all that bouncing, what a surprise it would be for him. One moment he would find it in my pants, the next where my brain was supposed to be. If this kept up, the contents of my stomach would be in my pants soon, too.

As my plane finally began to descend, at about a thousand feet it broke through the clouds. In the distance I could see the airport—and then it was gone again, the cloud having caught up with me. The turbulence was terrible. I had to get lower. Another hundred feet down, I was out of the cloud again, and the airport closer than before, but barely in line or sufficiently close for a landing.

Then the cloud caught up again.

On a normal approach, an airplane has to circle the

airport counter-clockwise to come in for a landing. I don't want to annoy you with the technical reasons for that. But at that moment, only a "direct," not a normal, approach could save me.

Finally, after continuously playing cat-and-mouse with the cloud and fighting the turbulence, I was only eight hundred feet high. And as if through a miracle, this time the turbulence and the cloud did not follow, and I had an unexpected breather. The airport elevation is six hundred feet, so I had only two hundred feet between me and the ground.

OK. I lowered the flaps. I throttled the engine. The descending speed settled to sixty-five knots. The airplane was a little to the right, so I made some alignment adjustments. The runway was then straight in front of me and all aligned. The grass before the runway started rushing past under me; I was about twenty feet above it. Finally the runway was under me, and I pulled the yoke back to flare out. Five feet of height to go, good, nice, right along the white center line of the runway, very good.

Then I heard a deafening screech and a louder shriek from the speaker, and I was overtaken by the impact of the crash.

You forgot to put your wheels down! flashed on my home computer screen. Oh, well, I thought. Can't win every time.

The home computer reset the Flight Simulator, and . . . It was a sunny early morning, and I was sitting in the cockpit of the Cessna, ready for takeoff. I wanted to practice flying cross-country to a small airport about fifty miles away.

So what has this Flight Simulator game I played on my computer to do with my real flight lessons on a Cessna at Spring Valley Airport?

Nothing—I just thought I would mention it to you.

BOY, WAS IT COLD!

YESTERDAY MORNING, AS I DO each day, I had the TV morning news on while still in bed, and the weatherman reported the outside temperature was 20 degrees and the wind-chill factor was "in the teens."

Daily, when I get up, I just hang a rope around me (sorry, I mean a robe; a rope would be too skimpy, don't you think?) and go outside for my newspaper, which is delivered in the driveway during the night. My wife told me, "I'm cold. Dress better."

I said, "I know it's twenty degrees outside, but I have on the top of my pajamas and a robe, and I'll be right back."

As I bent over and picked up the newspaper, a wind gust lifted my robe and pajama top and rolled them up exactly like a rope on my body. That wind-chill froze my back in an instant, and I could not get up anymore. I was frozen solid, half bent over, with the newspaper bag in my hand. My hand was trembling from the cold, so badly you could hear the paper rattling around in the bag.

Luckily, my wife was looking out the window and realized what was happening, and she knew right away what to do. She came running out with her hairdryer to blow warm air at me and heat me up so I could defrost. But she had to run back inside to get an extension cord. The electrical cord of the dryer was too short to reach any of the electrical outlets.

Finally, after the warm air of the hair dryer thawed me enough to move again and take the newspaper with me, I turned toward the kitchen door—but realized my wife was not behind me.

When I turned back, *she* was now frozen solid, standing there in the wind. I jumped back to her and grabbed the hairdryer, which she still had pointing in the direction I had needed it, and tried to turn it in her direction, so the warm air could blow at her and thaw her.

She screamed, "You're breaking my *arm!*" so I had to blow warm air through my mouth at the arm with all of my lung capacity, so I could thaw it enough to turn the dryer.

Then I again turned to go inside. When I got to the kitchen door, I realized that she had left it open in her hurry to help me, and to my horror there were already some icicles hanging on the kitchen faucet.

Finally, we were both back in the house, and the door was shut. Now the heat in the house could build up again, and we got warm, and the faucet, too—the ice was gone, and the faucet working again (I have to fix that faucet when it's warmer, but that's another story).

When I was warmed up, I took the newspaper out of the bag to read it, and would you believe—the newspaper was snow-white and blank! The newspaper had lost every letter because I had been shaking out there so hard from the cold with the newspaper bag in my hand. The letters had slid off the paper right into the plastic paper bag, so, naturally, I poured the letters out of the bag onto the table.

Now we had an enormous puzzle in front of us. My wife and I started gluing the letters back on the paper. Subsequently, wanting to know if we had pieced the stories together correctly, I went to a store and got another newspaper to see how well we had done.

I must say, our results were not too good; besides all the spelling mistakes we'd made, the stories did not match. In our paper, the President was resigning from his job; in the store paper, he'd gotten a $2-trillion budget approved. In our paper, the war was over; in the store paper, more troops had been sent to Afghanistan. In our paper, all politicians had from now on to hold only one job—no double dipping. Nothing like this was in the store paper. You get the idea. Should this happen again, I think I will have to enlist a newspaper editor to correct me. One thing I know—I sure will not go and pick up the paper when it is that cold with a robe (or rope) on from now on. I'll wait till summer!

Now I know why so many papers are lying around in so many driveways and are never picked up. All of these homeowners must not have a rope to put on to be warm enough.

CAREFREE

I'M IN MY EIGHTIES. I CAN admit that openly now because I'm "carefree." You see, I was constantly worried: Will I be on time, what will people say, have I paid my bills, what will I have to fix today—everything is worries, worries, and nothing going smoothly.

My wife always said, "You worry too much. Relax. Don't care so much. You're retired—feel free, it will be OK." But I turn around, and the worries just come back by themselves.

So, the other day, I had to buy some groceries—my wife was going somewhere and had given me instructions: sliced pork, eggs, potatoes, breadcrumbs, and, oh, yeah, onions (my favorite), and left. Later, when I looked at the clock, I thought, Ugh! I almost forgot to go to the store. So I worried again, Will I be home before her? Then, in the store, after I got the groceries, I got carried away and looked around some more.

Then it hit me: *What are you doing?* I have to get home before her or I will get a kick in my pants! (That's what she always threatens me with.) I turned into an aisle with diapers in it as a shortcut, an aisle I normally don't enter, but, though I rushed, I was blocked there again and again.

Wrong move; there were so many women there, the store must have been running some special sale. Then I saw it! A woman was grabbing a box with the legend *Carefree* on it in big letters. That was all. I had to see what in that box must be making her feel carefree. . .I will get one too, I thought, and I won't care anymore—no more worries! Yes, that's what I need! That's what my wife says. It must be in this box!

I pushed another woman out of my way who was eyeing the box, too; obviously she must also be the worrying kind. I grabbed the box, put it under my arm, and, *Ha!* There must be some wizardry in this box, I said to myself—I didn't even have to open it, and I was, in an instant, just carefree!

When I paid, the girl at the cash register looked at the box, then at me, kind of oddly (maybe I looked good to her, I thought—she must have liked my gray hair. . .or maybe not).

So what? I was carefree now; why worry? and I left.

When my wife got home, she said, "Do you know what's in this box? What did you buy it for? I don't need it anymore."

"I know you don't need it, because you're already carefree. I'm the one who had to worry all the time, and I don't want to know what's in this box. It works for me because it made me feel carefree."

Since then, whenever I go somewhere, I tuck that box

under my arm, and I'm instantly feeling carefree. I just don't understand why my wife doesn't want to go shopping, or out with me, anymore.

Do you know why? If you do, tell me.

Epilogue: I finally opened the box. I could find nothing but what looked like eye shields, for when you want to have a carefree slumber and the light is too bright. It was a big letdown. Now I worry again.

CHANGES IN MY LIFETIME
1931-2002 AND 2013

I N 2002, I WAS APPROACHING seventy-one years of age and thinking about what had changed in my lifetime. If one of my old dead relatives came back for one day, they would not know what to do with all these new appliances and gladly go back to being dead again.

In the kitchen, there was no refrigerator, no microwave, electric or gas stove, and all these kitchen gadgets like toasters, can openers, and blenders. We were fairly advanced: We had an icebox; once a week, the iceman came, drained the water, and put a block of ice into a compartment in the middle of the unit.

How about a toaster? At snack time, bread was toasted on the top of the kitchen stove, which was a wood-burner; then the toast was rubbed with garlic, and some pork fat or butter was spread on it. (Can you believe this? Fat, butter, daily, and I'm still alive!) If you cooked a meal, you had to add wood to the stove at least three times before the food was cooked. Coffee and tea were made on the stove too, and the milk had to be boiled, since there was no pasteurization then. Can openers? There were no cans, so no need for one of those. Blenders? If something had to be blended, you used a bowl, a fork, and elbow grease. Microwaves? Say that again? For heaven's sake, World War II was still eight years in the future.

TV! Never heard of it. Tape player? Never heard of it. DVD, video, CD player? Never heard of them. Come to think of it, did the people when you were born know what a DVD or video player was, or a computer? Gramophone player? Oh, yes, that we had. Radio? When I was about five years old, my father bought the first one for us, and you could hear several stations.

With the radio, I remember a little story. The family was sitting and listening to some music on the new radio. My great-grandmother was visiting us and listened to the music, too. The next day, my mother and I happened to enter the room where the radio was. My great-grandmother was turning the station dial up and down, never stopping long enough to hear what was on a station. "What are you doing, Grandma?" my mother asked.

"Oh, I'm looking for the music we listened to yesterday." Understanding a gramophone, where you had just to play the record over again, she thought the radio did the same as long you dialed the right station.

We had the radio about a week. In order to plug it into an outlet (there were not too many outlets in the house, no need for them then), the electrical cord had to go over a doorway. If you wanted to go into the next room, you had to unplug the cord or lift your leg over it. I was told to watch out for this, so nothing would happen to the radio till an electrician installed another outlet closer to the radio. This job was not so easy, since the walls were all brick and had to be chiseled open and then plastered again.

I did my best to not to trip over the cord, but my foot did not go high enough. The radio did not quite survive; it went flying in one direction, some parts in the other, and I lengthwise. The radios at that time were monstrous and heavy. How I got ours back up on the shelf again was a puzzle to my parents for a long time. And what happened to me? That I have not forgotten all this time, and I still don't understand it—it was nothing. I had almost died from fright, and then nothing! The radio got fixed, and not much was said to me. (But the pain from the fall I had—what a killer that was.)

There is another story of a new gadget in 1935. The clothing irons at that time were heated by charcoal, a lengthy process. My father bought my mother the first electrical iron in the neighborhood. So, naturally, all the women came to see how it worked. One of my friends was a year older than I, and we were both watching the demonstration, too. My mother plugged the iron into the outlet, and, with lot of oohs and ahs, it got hot, and she could iron a dress.

This was a big demonstration for my friend and me. When everybody left, we decided to play Electric Iron. He took two hairpins, put one into each hand, and he was the electrical cord; I was the iron and put my arms around his belly. Then he put the two hairpins into the outlet.

The next thing we knew, we were both flying under the kitchen table! The poor guy had burns on his hands, and what happen to the hairpins I don't know. All I had was a tremendous headache from hitting the table with my head when we were thrown through the air. Believe me, don't ever play Electric Iron; I never did again.

Seventy years later, I am eighty-two. There are computers with a hundred thousand gigabytes of hard memory. My first computer, a Commodore 64, had sixty-four thousand kilobytes. At the beginning of around 1983, my second computer, a Vic Junior, had 128—*ohh*, so many kilobytes, and you could save some of your own creations, too. I will never use up this memory. Now, the telephone you have in your pocket, not only to talk with, but to take pictures and play radio and TV, are a thousand times stronger than my first computer. Soon cars will be driving themselves.

I won't be here much longer, and, believe me, I will not come back to all this mess again. No way; it's yours.

CHEESEFLY

TWO OF MY GRANDCHILDREN, Mary Anna and Joseph (both in their twenties), were visiting my wife and me. There is always a lot of talking on these occasions about this and that.

For whatever reason I did not grasp, my wife read to them a story about butterflies, and they seemed very interested. I could not stay out of *that*, could I? So I waited till she was finished and had left.

Then I went to the refrigerator and looked for a stick of butter. I could not find any, but there were some slices of cheese. So I took a slice and walked to the table where the grandchildren were sitting.

I said to them, "I wanted to demonstrate how the butterfly flies, but I couldn't find any butter to demonstrate, so I have to show you how a cheesefly flies," and I threw the cheese in the air. It just missed my grandson—he ducked under the table.

Believe me, my story sure was more interesting than a butterfly, and they broke out in laughter, and if they have not stopped by now, they're still laughing.

This is someway to be remembered when I'm gone, is it not?

CLOTHES I LIKED

THERE ARE SOME CLOTHES I remember that I really liked at the time I wore them, but one outfit—if you can call it clothes at all—I still have. Here's the story behind it.

I always feel cold, at least nine months of the year. The average person hollers,"It's so hot today," when it's just a little over seventy-five degrees. For me, ninety and up is when I start to like the weather; close to a hundred for me is still OK. Seventy-five is too low—I feel cold and freezing at sixty-eight.

About five years ago, I was complaining how cold it was at sixty-eight and put more and more clothing on. My wife always insists that it is still really warm. I guess in her mind this is not the only disagreement between us to come up sometimes. She says that I'm wrong many times, but this is only in her mind, of course. I know when I'm right.

That day, as I shivered and complained how cold I felt, it overcame the usual tolerance of her mind. She grabbed a four-by-five-foot blanket we had bought a few days before, snuck up behind me, opened it up, and threw it over my head—I guess so she could not hear me complaining anymore. It really surprised me, but it seemed to make me instantly warmer.

But I want see too, and the blanket was covering my face. I took it off, and then folded it in half and in quarters, and cut the corner off the fold. When I opened it, there was a hole in the middle of the blanket. My wife saw this and almost fainted. "What did you do with this *blanket?*" she hollered.

"I'll show you—watch me," I said. I rolled half the blanket up so the hole was still open, then threw the blanket up in the air, and when it came down, my head went through the hole and the blanket landed on my shoulders, covering half my body. "See? Next time you throw this blanket over me, at least I'll be able to see, too."

It was the first time I had ever been able to leave my wife speechless—what a surprise that was for me! Normally, she has the last word.

But the cut edge of the blanket had these little unraveled fibers that were really irritating my neck. I set up the sewing machine and ran a hem around the cut. I know—you want to know why I did this hemming, and not my wife. It was my creation, I told myself, and if I let her do it, she'll tell everybody it was hers and steal all the admiration I'll get for it! Ha, no! Doing it is me, mine, and nobody else's. I wanted to hear how smart I was.

But I have to admit she had a name for it. "This is a poncho and nothing else."

"Well, call it what you want, a poncho or a ponchomami, it does the trick, it keeps me warm. And you can have all my clothes and put them on yourself, but you will never get the poncho! It is mine."

Then I asked her, really sweetly, "Do you want me to make one, a really nice one, for you, too?"

"No!" she barked, so you see, our minds did match that time. I really didn't want to make another one anyway.

CRAZY THING I'VE DONE

WHEN I WAS ABOUT seven, we were new in town. My father had relocated with his family, for business reasons, to a different town, and had rented an apartment next to an inn.

The inn had a big yard, and we neighborhood kids played in this yard a lot with some dogs from the inn, balls, and so on—what boys like to play.

One day, I was alone there for awhile, and while I was playing by myself with a ball because no other kids were around, I had to go to the bathroom.

The four toilets were connected on the back wall of the inn, with a men's room on the side. The toilets each had walls and a door, but the men's room had walls and no door. It was open in the front, with slatted concrete flooring at a lower angle to the wall and a hole to the cesspool.

I know you're thinking, Why the heck do I have to know all this? Please excuse me, but I was asked about a crazy thing that I've done, so stay here and don't go away.

I had just gone to the toilet next to this men's room when I heard a man entering the room, and I got interested in how he was doing his business.

I climbed on a two-by-four nailed to the wall; when I stood on it, I could look down through a space between the wall and the ceiling. I was shocked at the size of this man, and I'm not talking about his height. I ran to my mother and told her what I'd seen. To this day, I don't know if she was amused or angry. She got really red in the face and scolded me for breaking into somebody's private time.

When my father came home, she told him my story. Just imagine—she had told me not to break into somebody's private time, but she had just divulged what I had told her in a private communication.

My father grumbled what a bad boy I was and grabbed a broom in the kitchen. This was a real shock to me—He's never hollered at me before, I thought, and now he goes for a broom?

Out the door I ran. Oh, dear God! He was still after me. I ran faster than fast, and he could not catch up with me—at least that was what I was thinking then.

Another time I heard him talking in the other room. My ears were wide open: I was breaking into somebody's private conversation again! Oh, what a bad kid I was; I was so ashamed.

He was telling a story to his buddies about what I had done at a card game in the inn, and all of his friends found it hilarious.

Then one friend went to the men's room and came back, telling them that he had looked up because of my story, and then was shocked himself, because there were two boys standing there watching him!"

I knew exactly why they were there. I'd told my story to the other boys, and they'd found it hilarious, too.

ELECTRICAL GUTTER

IN THE MIDDLE OF the 1930s, when we were living next to the inn in the town in Yugoslavia—a large, beautiful building with ivy covering its walls, which had a bar, a large dining room, several guest rooms for overnight guests, and a large back yard with stables for horses, cows, pigs, and poultry—a guest always had fresh milk, eggs, meat, and most of the food was prepared fresh by the inn.

The neighborhood children around the inn had a good time too, because there was always something to see, like cars, horse buggies, people, all the farm animals in the yard, and there were several dogs to play with, too.

And then there was the town drunk. When he came out of the inn, he was all over the sidewalk. I never did see him walk straight. We kids taunted him, although I don't think that he cared; he never acknowledged anything, nor did he seem to see us.

When he came out of the bar, he was stooped so far forward that he had to run so his feet could catch up with his nose. As soon the feet caught up, his upper body swayed back, and then the feet were suddenly too far ahead. One step back, a quarter turn of his body, three more steps to the side, and his head and feet were in balance for another split second again. These acrobatic maneuvers went on until he was home, about a block and a half away. I must admit, I never did see him fall.

One day we watched him come out of the inn, doing his usual maneuvers. This time, whether it was to steady himself or to take a rest, he stretched his hand out to lean on the gutter of the inn leading from the roof, down along the wall to the sidewalk. As soon as his hand touched that gutter, he screamed, "Ooh, yeow! *Help!*" With one hand holding on to the gutter, his other hand started punching the air. Then it was whirling like a windmill, and the screams! No banshee could have matched them.

Now this was new! It had all our attention in a second. Half astounded, half amused, we congregated in a half circle around this new show. Finally, an older boy asked what the matter was and grabbed the drunk by the hand. The next moment he was with the drunk in synchronized hollering. This was spooky—some of the kids took off, some stayed. They were probably, just as I was, unable to move.

After a couple more twitches, the drunk and the boy fell to the ground free of the gutter. The drunk was up instantly and, to our astonishment, ran home straight as an arrow. The boy, however, swayed like a drunk, screaming for his mother. A man came out of the inn to see what this was all about, touched the gutter, jumped back with a yelp, and declared the gutter was charged with electricity.

Now that we knew that no spook was involved, we got brave. In the back yard of the inn was a dog named Shecky; when we yelled rat and pointed to a hole, the dog would go wild and start digging, barking, and so forth. The game could go on for an hour, and the dog did not get tired.

We called Shecky, who came with his tail wagging until we showed him the gutter and said, "Rat." The friendly dog turned instantly into an attacking wolf. As his wet nose touched the gutter, Shecky got a jolt. He jumped five feet straight up in to the air! This went so fast, you could not even see his legs move.

He started yapping.

On the way down, Shecky must have decided that the rat had bitten him. More furious than ever, he attacked again. This time he jumped not up but back, yipped loudly, and bowled over a kid. Once more he approached the gutter, this time carefully; he looked in the hole, walked from one side to the other, then sniffed, and his nose touched. Just like the kid and the drunk, he took off yelping. We were laughing so hard that our stomachs were hurting. Poor Shecky was no fun for quite a few days after that; if somebody showed him a hole and said, "Rat," he just walked away.

Many people passing by got talked into touching the gutter. Everybody had to try at least once, knowingly or unknowingly. The kids got all the dogs in the neighborhood together. Soon there were a bunch of adults, kids, dogs, screaming, yelling, yelping, snarling, jumping, and running.

Then Hans had an idea: How about Mimi the cow? He led her out of the stable. When Mimi's nose touched the gutter, she took off with Hans just able to get hold of her tail. Probably sure by then that the devil was after her, Mimi galloped down the street. Hans, holding on for dear life, was half flying, half running. His steps were so large that a kangaroo could have learned something from him. Mimi and Hans disappeared around the corner. The rest of us were all on the floor, laughing.

I know, nowadays, this would be looked at as cruelty to animals. But in reality, no dog, cow, or human got really hurt. I know because I touched the gutter too, and later in life got zapped by much more powerful currents without damage. As it happened, an evergreen had grown over the gutter on the roof and the electrical wiring to the house. The electrical wiring at that time had no insulation outside the houses or in the streets, so when the evergreen touched the wire and the gutter, it charged the latter. The gutter did not touch the ground either, so anybody on the ground touching the gutter and grounding it out got a shock. After the evergreen was cut, the gutter was safe.

The drunk, Shecky, and the gutter are long gone, but in my memory they still live on, and when my grandchildren see me lost in thought and smiling they say: "Probably he's thinking of Shecky. Let's get out of here before we have to listen to that story again."

MY HOW-BIG-THE-FISH-WAS STORY

YOU KNOW THE FISHY stories told by fisherman about the big one that gets away all the time after being caught? A long time ago, *I* was the fish that got away and didn't get caught.

I went, as I do almost every day, for a walk in the Mahwah Campgaw Reservation in Bergen County, New Jersey. One day on my walk, I met two men and two women who were very excited as they were passing me. They told me to watch out because they had seen a bear in the woods. This was not big news to me. I had seen one some time before, walking in the distance, too. The bear just did not pay any attention to me and went his way.

So I just walked a little off the trails into the woods. Suddenly, there was the bear—maybe forty yards in front of me. This one did not run; it approached even closer. It stopped about fifty feet in front of me and lifted itself up on its hind legs, clawing and beating with its front legs the air, and made all kinds of terrible noises.

What to do? Instantly, I was so scared I was ready to go on the toilet, but I had no toilet paper with me, so this was out of question. I knew I could not outrun the bear with my heavy boots on.

Then it occurred to me—maybe the bear is a female.

So I turned around, pulled my pants down, and mooned it. Lo and behold, it *was* a female, and in womanly fashion she covered her eyes with her paws. Luckily, she had no fingers to peek through like a human female would and could not see me anymore. So I was able to sneak away and write this story for you.

(Now I wonder how long she remained there with her eyes covered up.)

This is the end of my fishy bear story.

It's the absolute truth, I swear. And if you believe it, I have some more I can tell you. . . .

Interested?

GASOLINE PRICES

HOW DID GAS PRICES get to be so high? Say the price is $2.80 a gallon. The oil companies have a meeting and decide the price is too low.

First company: "We have to lift the price a minimum ten cents a gallon."

Second company: "Are you nuts? Twenty-five cents would be just right."

Third company: "Hey, you guys, wake up! We need a fifty-cent raise."

Fourth company: "Now—if we raise the price fifty cents to $3.20, everybody will complain."

First company: "Since they complain anyway, why not make it $3.50?"

Second company: "That's right. We have to do something, but what?"

All companies together: "That's simple—we go up over $4.50. The complaint is there anyway. Then we go down after a while to $3.50, and everybody has forgotten $2.80 and is happy with the $3.50—why, they think it's a bargain!"

That's the way the ball bounces—

All oil companies agree.

Now the oil companies are happy.
The entire country is happy.
And you're happy, too.
Right?
So what do you want, more than that?
(Myself, I want the $1.00 a gallon back)

    P. S. The auto industry is happy too when gas prices go down. When the people are happy, they buy the bigger cars again. This makes the gas companies even happier, because bigger cars have bigger tanks, and thus there's a chance to sell even more gas.

And the oil companies are happy too—that is, until one of the oil bosses wants another house and a diamond ring for his wife. Then it all starts over again

Just read from the start.

GOING TO KINDERGARTEN!

MY GRANDDAUGHTER MARY ANNA has had anxiety for the last six weeks because she has to go to kindergarten this year. Her parents, and the rest of the family, try to cheer her up and tell her how nice it is and how many new friends she will make. There's only one week left before the start of kindergarten, and the distress is great enough to bring her to tears. "Grandpa," she cries, "I don't want to go."

"But look at all the fun you'd miss out on if you don't! And you're such a cute little girl, all the kids who will want to be your friends would miss out if you don't go," I tell her.

"Well, I know I'm cute, and you know I'm cute, but how will the kids know that?" she asks.

"Because you are. Besides, look at it this way—if you don't go to kindergarten, you can't go to school next year," I pointed out.

This was the wrong answer. I knew it as soon as the words were out of my mouth, when her face brightened and she joyfully told me: "Hey, this is just right! I don't want to go to first grade either."

What are grandfathers for? To cheer up their grand-children, right?

I myself hated kindergarten so immensely that I can still remember it today. The hard time I had, and my granddaughter has, with kindergarten must be in our genes. My poor mother had to take me by the hand daily and literally drag me to kindergarten because I did not want to go.

Finally, she'd had enough. She grabbed a wooden spoon. "Now," she said, "either you go to kindergarten by yourself, or I'll use the wooden spoon." Normally the threat of the wooden spoon brought me in line very fast. But here was a choice—wooden spoon or kindergarten—and, while the wooden spoon hurt for a little while, I figured, kindergarten hurt all day. So I told my mother, "Wooden spoon."

Later in life I found out that my mother realized at that instant how much I must have hated kindergarten. Giving in was not possible, so she said, "You will take the spoon? Not only will I give you the spoon, but you will get it all the way to the kindergarten." With this I got a good whack on my behind, and by the time she lifted her arm for the second whack, I was out the door.

As soon as I felt safe, I slowed down. Kaboom!—another whack out of the blue. She really was behind me. Like oiled lightning, I ran out of the yard and into the street, and when I glanced behind me, the shadow of my mother was still there. As we ran down the street, I cried,

"I don't want to go!"

My mother hollered, "You *will* go," swinging her wooden spoon over her head, ready to whack me again.

I don't know if anybody saw this performance, but we must have looked like two characters stepping out of a newspaper cartoon. To me, of course, she seemed a goddess of doom swinging a sword over her head for the awful purpose of taking my head off.

At the end of the block, my mother, convinced I'd gotten the message, turned around and went home. I ran a little further, then, realizing she was gone, turned around and went home too. I stuck my head in the door and asked quite innocently, "Are you still angry? Can I stay home now?"

If you want to know what followed just go back and reread from the first whack, with the difference that she ran after me *all* the way to the kindergarten. After about a week of this, I did not need the spoon; I was finally broken, and I went by myself without a fight.

The teacher had not much to complain of about me; actually, she told my mother I was a little on the quiet side and followed instructions well. This made my mother wonder if she was talking about me or somebody else. But the teacher did not know me yet.

The school was in a new building and a bit off the main way. For whatever reason, there was only a narrow concrete walkway; the rest of the side road going to the building was still dirt, so when it rained it got very messy.

Once, after a downpour, the teacher did not want to let us go home until the water had run off a little. At the same time, she wanted to teach us a lesson, and declared, "You kids were not behaving today. Everybody has to stay in class as punishment."

What? Stay over? Wasn't the school day too long as it was? Had I heard right—punishment? What did I do? I'd been good all day, I wanted to ask her; why are you punishing me? It went against my belief in righteousness and law and order. The time was ripe for the teacher to learn something about me, too.

I simply got up from my seat and started toward the door. "Where do you think you're going?" she asked me.

"Oh. I want to see if it's still raining." I reached the door, opened it, and left.

"Hey, come back!" she shouted. There was no going back. I was going home. She could shout as much as she wanted to.

Hey, what's this? She was running after me, like my mother. But if I could outrun my mother, no teacher was going to catch me.

I sprinted as fast as I could, but somehow she was catching up. There was only one thing to do: run across the muddy road.

The first step surprised me—how slippery the mud was! On the second step, mud filled my shoes, and by the third I was knee-deep in it, but that didn't stop me. I reached the other side. Where was the teacher? Likely propelled forward by too much speed, she'd landed in the mud, too. Her second step went as far as my third, and there she was standing, with her mouth wide open and no sound, up to her shin-bones in mud.

At that moment, I must admit, I had the greatest admiration for her—even my mother would not have gone so far for me.

The best was yet to come, when she turned around. The mud was, as I said, very slippery—one foot went this way, the other that way, and there she was, sitting down with a splash, which was Olympic gold-medal worthy. I don't want to burden you with what she said, or screamed, after that. I just ran home.

How did I get back to the kindergarten again? Both my parents had to come in for a conference. For some reason I did not have to go to kindergarten for a week. I was probably the first human who got suspended from kindergarten. After that, the wooden spoon had to do its duty for another week. My wish was that there would be another rainy day, since I was sure I could get another week off.

I hope my two grandsons, coming up in due time for kindergarten too, have not inherited this gene. Otherwise, good luck to my daughter and daughter-in-law when it happens.

HAVING A TEA?

I did sit down to have a
Tea
In the shadow of a
Tree,
But I did not see the
Bee.
She stung me on the
Knee.
It hurts so much, I think I have to
Pee.
Now I stand here as you
See
And scream, "Oh, why? Oh, why, could it not
Be
That she sting somebody else but
Me?"
Along comes Grandma and
She
Says it will pass, the pain soon will
Flee.
"How about I make you a nice cup of
Tea?

Now don't go back to the beginning of this story—
this has to
End.
Please don't tear this paper, fold, or
Bend.

Just lay it
Away
And have a nice
Day.

HENRY, MY FRIEND

I MET HENRY FOR THE first time in 1965, when I was working on a new addition to my house and he came over to take a look. I'd lived there for six years, and Henry had lived in his house across the street for about two. Although neighbors all this time, we had never met before. Little did I know then that, on that day, a friendship would start that has lasted a lifetime!

Henry and I are, so to speak, in many ways on the same wavelength. We've gone fishing, bowling, and flying a couple times in a small airplane, and we have taken our wives to the movies, to Manhattan, down to the shore to swim, and on sled rides. Besides, our wives have gotten to be just as good friends as we are, which did not change even after Henry and Nancy sold their house and bought another somewhere else. When Henry purchased a second house on the shore, we went boating and crabbing, too.

As you probably know, people who go bowling have to take their shoes off and put on bowling sneakers. After bowling once, Henry and I put our shoes back on and went home. My wife asked me, "When did you buy those shoes? I've never seen them on you."

I had no idea. Then the phone rang. "Hello?"

It was Henry. "Hey," he said, "you've got my shoes on."

"Well," I said, "if I've got your shoes on, then you've got mine," and that was the answer to my wife's question, too.

Another time, *Star Trek II* was playing in the movies. Our wives were not interested in going. I was working quite a bit of overtime then, and I was really tired, but I wanted to see it. So did Henry, and we went. The theater was not too full; we took our seats in the middle. Henry was sitting on my left; on my right was an empty seat, and somebody else was sitting in the next.

I suddenly woke up. Henry was gone, and there was nobody sitting on my right, either. I had the whole aisle to myself, and then I discovered that, not only that aisle, but all the others nearby, were empty, too.

Where is Henry? I wondered, and turned around to see him sitting four aisles back. With that, the lights came on, and everybody got up. It dawned on me I must have slept through the movie. On my way out, when I caught up with Henry, I asked, "What happened?"

"You snored so loud that everybody started looking at you and me, so I told them, 'I don't know this guy,' and moved away. So did everybody else sitting around you."

To this day I haven't seen *Star Trek II.*

Just when the motion picture industry came out with the new movie ratings—PG, R, X, and XXX, there was an

X-rated movie playing at the Bergen Mall that our wives did not want to go to, so Henry and I decided to go ourselves. We only made one mistake. We did not check in the newspaper for the name of the film—but since it was X rated, who cared?

Here I want to point out it was not XXX rated; otherwise, we would not have gone either—naturally. (My wife says, "You would have run!" Oh, yeah? It just goes to show how little she knows me.)

We bought the tickets and, halfway into the film, Henry said, "I think we're in the wrong film."

"I don't understand," I replied. "It said Bergen Mall."

"Are we *in* the Bergen Mall?"

I told you before that Henry and I are on the same wave length. Here is the proof; in the same instant we both discovered we had made a mistake. We were not only seeing the wrong film, but in the wrong mall—it was the Garden State Plaza.

Out we went to the Bergen Mall and into the right film.

At the end of this film we knew we would have been better off staying in the first one. One thing we are still wondering: Should we have asked for our money back when we discovered we were in the wrong movie?

Another day, I was driving home with Henry on Route 59 in Rockland County, New York. When the route enters Suffern, there is a monument to the Unknown Soldier. The street around this monument is a one-way circle. To get where I wanted to go, I would have to drive around the monument. I was talking to Henry and turned absent-mindedly in the wrong direction of the one-way circle.

Who enters a one-way circle the wrong way? Only a guy like me who has gotten absorbed in a conversation. A police car (tell me where they are when you need them!) immediately entered the circle in the correct direction. Since there was only room for one car-width, the police car had to stop and back up to let me go past.

To make this story short, Henry and I had to pool our money together to bail me out. Several days later, I got a lecture and a stiff fine from a judge. That's when I swore to myself, I will never talk to Henry again. . .while I drive.

One day, I helped Henry to redo some stairs on his garage. We bought all the lumber, and all went as planned until we discovered that we needed another six-foot piece of two-by-four lumber. We drove to Channel's in Ramsey to buy it. Here the little devil got the best of us again. We picked up the two-by-four, Henry one end, I the other end, put it on our shoulders, and marched through the store with Henry leading.

Picture this: Two not-so-young men walking through the store, on their shoulders a single piece of lumber that a four-year-old could have carried. Surprise, amazement and laughter from other shoppers followed us, one guy said, "Need some help, fellows?"

We assured him we could handle it.

The cashier-lady got eyes as big as hamburgers; you

could see she was not sure whether she should be afraid and run, or was this some kind of fun? Still unsure how to take us, she worked the cash register with lightning speed just to get us out. She peeped, in a barely audible voice, "One dollar twenty-nine, please."

After we paid, we shouldered our two-by-four again and walked out of the store. At the door, I looked around; the cashier was gripping the counter and looked ready to faint. I turned to Henry and said; "I figure this was my last time in this store."

He answered, "Mine, too."

And so be it till the next time.

A Holyday Dinner

SOMETHING UNUSUAL OCCURRED ONE day at a dinner we had while I was still a very young kid living in Yugoslavia. My great-grandparents had invited my family, and some uncles and aunts and all their children, for something similar to a Thanksgiving dinner at their house. We were about twenty-five to thirty people in all.

On occasions like that, there was always some major cooking by my great-grandmother and her housemaid. We were all seated in the dining room, and were served some pork, some beef, and a broiled goose, with wine and all kinds of drinks, including grape juice and sodas for the children.

The town had a population of around thirty-two thousand. On its outskirts, several hundred Gypsies were living. They went begging from house to house many times, and there was a extra lot of begging when there was a holyday.

We were waiting for my great-grandfather, who was always the last one to sit down, to say a prayer. The custom then was that no one ate before that. When he had finished his prayer and we were about to eat, we heard a knock on the door.

Puzzled, my great-grandfather shouted, "Come in." Our visitor was a Gypsy. He saw us sitting at a table loaded with food and must have had the goose in his eye.

He started out with a cock-a-doodle-doo, crowing like rooster, took a step and crowed, another step and crowed, and soon enough he was close to the table. He jumped toward it, grabbed the goose, and ran like hell out the door. Everybody started hollering, and one uncle jumped up to follow him.

But my great grandfather barked, "Stop! Let him go. Do you want to eat what this guy had in his hand? . . . We still have plenty of food for everybody here—we don't need that. Cock-a-doodle-doo!" he continued. "We should start eating now."

This broke the ice, and everybody started to laugh. My great-grandfather added then, "Let this poor soul have the best meal he will ever have, and let us start eating what we have."

There were all kinds of funny stories after that, thanks to the Gypsy, for the rest of the day. And everybody, and especially us kids, practiced the cock-a-doodle-doo to a perfection.

HOW DID WE GET
TO CELEBRATE BIRTHDAYS?

W AY BACK IN TIME, there was this not-too-bright king who always forgot how old he was. When he went to a doctor or somebody else asked him, he never got it right. Sometimes two or three years passed before he added another year to his age, and this eventually made him ten years younger than he really was.

When he reached fifty, he was saying he was thirty-nine, and there he stayed (you know people do it still—I don't have to tell you that). This was very annoying to the doctors and the authorities. They aged, but not the king; oh, no, he was always only thirty-nine!

So what to do? Somebody came up with the idea of giving him a birthday party, to remind him that he was a year older, but this had to be very carefully orchestrated. Nobody wanted to lose his head over it.

When the king reached fifty-five, and they celebrated it and were singing to him,"Happy fifty-fifth birthday to you, happy fifty-fifth birthday to you,"to make certain he remembered, they also sang,"How old are you now?" And just to be assured he knew, they repeated the song until he said, "I'm fifty-five now. Please stop—I will remember."

From then on, every year this was repeated, so he did understand for sure how old he was. Before you know it, this got to be a tradition for every person, because they realized it was good for business. You know!

Birthday equals cards, cake, flowers, toys, and gifts. How can business go wrong?

So don't get fooled: There is only one birthday in your life; all the other so-called birthdays are just a reminder that another year's gone by.

(And, yes, it's good for business too—and don't forget it.)

That is why we celebrate birthdays.

It is money! Some for you, and a lot for the stores!

So now you know what happiness and birthdays are all about.

I know, you don't agree with me about this story. That's fine. Just don't beat me up. Enjoy your birthday.

THE HAPPY BIRTHDAY WISHES
ALWAYS ARE

EVERY TIME SOMEBODY HAS a birthday, people wish them a happy birthday, and good luck, and "much happiness in the future."

But there's not much you can do about having good luck. You can try for it, but you may have it only sometimes, or maybe not at all.

What about happiness? To be happy, you can do something. Then what about those jibs and jabs that occur in life and makes you so unhappy?

There's also nothing much you can do about them; jibs and jabs do come. But look at it this way: You can learn something from them that can make you happy later. Make something good out of unhappy moments by learning how to do better next time. Then, when something bad comes up again, you will not be feeling so down.

Always remember too that, no matter how bad something is, somebody has it worse than you—and, in a while, it will not be so bad anymore, and maybe even will be forgotten.

So remember the happy moments in your life, and let the bad ones be bygones. This can make you a very happy person indeed—and then you'll even have good luck.

HOW I GOT MY DRIVER'S LICENSE

O H MY, OH MY—that was in 1949. I was about eighteen and still living in Salzburg, working as an apprentice in the automobile repair shop. To know how to drive was a necessity, although I did not own a car. But that is another story.

How long ago is this? . . . From the '40s to the '50s, one finger, is ten years; then the '60s are another finger, the '70s, '80s, '90s. . .you figure out the rest, I'm out of fingers. It's 2013 now, and to remember all that I really have to think.

The license for driving in Austria was awarded in three categories: "A" for motorcycles, "B" for cars, and "C" for trucks, which was what I needed (no bus or train or airplane license was ever required, thank God; I did not need that).

The requirements for getting any driver's license were available in a government agency, at which all the vehicles, including a teacher, were supplied. I think the whole program was free, paid for by public taxes.

"A": The motorcycles were BMWs that had, not two wheels, but three—the type you see in old war movies, like the ones the German army used. It had a sidecar the instructor sat in. If you've ever been on a bicycle or motor-cycle going around a curve, you know that you lean into the curve, but not on that type. It is more complicated: going to the left would lift the third wheel off the road (dangerous); going to the right was impossible, since the sidecar wheel wouldn't let you. So to get the license, you had, not only to take a normal driving test, but also be able to drive what looked like the figure eight on a steep, narrow hilly road. You started out in the middle of the road, drove to the right side, made a left turn around pass, through the middle where you were before, wound up on the left side (the former right side of the road), turned in the other direction, made a right turn around, and wound up in the same direction you were in to start before moving on. After practicing with the instructor for a few one-hour lessons I passed it and got my "A" license.

"B":The ordinary car driver's license was simpler. The cars at that time had no automatic transmission, no power steering, and no directional signals. The standard transmission had a clutch, so you had, not two, but three pedals: a gas, a brake, and clutch. On the right side of the car, the instructor also had a clutch and brake pedal, so if you did something wrong, he could override what you were doing.

Nowadays, you should always keep both hands on the wheel. But at that time, the law was that you had to use your left arm for directional signaling. An arm out of your open window, bent down at the elbow, meant you were slowing down or stopping. Stretching the arm straight out with an open hand-signaled a right turn. Pointing a stretching arm straight up meant a left turn. In the winter, you had to make sure your glove was really tightened down on your wrist, or the wind might blow it off, and then it would be hard to stop and go without it. If you've ever driven a standard transmission, you don't need an explanation of how to use a clutch; if not, just be happy.

"C": The truck took a little longer to manage, especially backing up, parking, and driving on streets, but at the driving test, I passed it too without a boo-boo to either the truck or me or, God forbid, to the instructor.

Another day, I had to go off to the office for some more verbal tests, written tests, and to have my picture taken to get the license. Finally after a day's work, I walked out with the license. At that time, the license was for life; you did not have to renew it ever unless you did something wrong and it was confiscated by the police. The last time I was in Austria in 1992, I'd already had my license for fifty years, and I was still able to rent and drive a car with it. I still have it and I'd like to show to you, but I put it somewhere and I have to find it first.

You asked about the license photo. I had been eighteen when it was taken, and didn't I ever need a new one? That's why I want you to see it. I'm now eighty-one, but if you switch the integers, I'm eighteen again! Anyhow, when I look in the mirror, I don't see a difference. I haven't changed or aged that much at all; I'm still me (my hair is just grayer).

When I came to the United State and started working on cars in a garage in Jeffersonville, New York, and I needed a New York license, my boss took me to Monticello, where I passed the driving and written test for cars somehow although my English was very poor at the time. I didn't need a motorbike or truck license, and what a relief that was! Now I have a New Jersey license, and I never ever lost any of them (points. . .well, sometimes). Obviously, I must be a good driver—at least that's what I think, even though I at times hear a horn behind me and can see somebody in another car pointing and talking to me through the window while I'm driving. I cannot hear what is said; I figure they must be congratulating me on my driving skills.

Only in the United States has there been the practice of license renewal, and a new picture taken, every four years—though this too has now changed. I had to renew my license this year and was able to do it by mail. As I said, I still look the same as an eighty-one/eighteen-year-old, so no picture taking was necessary.

SCIENCE MAGAZINES

W HEN I READ SOME of my science magazines, I find articles about how good medicine has gotten, and how it can kill almost all germs. How, lately, they say, there is not only our universe but maybe multiple universes in a kind of super-universe. I read about protons, atoms, positive matter, negative matter, billions of galaxies filled with billions of stars each. Huh. I shudder to think, where will this end? Did anybody ever wonder if there's life over there? If there is, are there duplicates, in these universes, of Earth, of me?

My reactions to these considerations veer off in different directions. Let me list them in turn.

1. How come all these scientists are so smart, yet none can tell me, if a doctor kills all of these germs, do they scream when they are dying? Or do they just lie on their backs, throw up their legs, and this is the end? Maybe they roll their eyes?

2. If a proton is circled by electrons, like a planet around a star, is this a solar system in miniature? If so, is, for example, my computer, with trillion of protons and electrons, a miniature universe like one they are talking

about? And is the mouse of the computer just another universe colliding with the computer to make pictures? If so, then each object you look at on the computer is from another universe!

3. Maybe if scientists found life on other planets in our universe, they would not have to wonder if life maybe exists in other universes, too—those universes which are nothing but galaxies in a super-universe. And then they would know if all these planets are just electrons in a much larger universe. If there is life elsewhere, are duplicates of me doing the same thing I'm doing at the moment I am doing it? Or is one of us a leader and the rest follow, or one a professor and the other a homeless version of me, and is that duplicate retired as I am? Questions after questions!

4. If there is life on another planet, what does intelligent life look like? You say you'd be able see it on some TV shows. Yes, but those characters look all too human. What if they have three heads with five eyes in each? Does this make them see better or smarter than us? With six arms and hands, do they need then help from somebody else to do anything? Does a doctor at an operation need the nurses to help, or do all of those arms operate by themselves? What if they have three wheels instead of two legs? They use helicopters, of course—no need to walk or roll. Have you thought about this? What if those three heads don't agree with each other? What if they have no heads, and all their brain is in their belly? (And then, if

they use a toilet, does this brain have a nose, or is it lost but renews itself in some way?).

How little we know. I'll keep on reading more magazines; maybe there will be an answer in one of them. What will I do then—stop reading?

HOW SOME TOWNS GOT THEIR NAMES

MANY YEARS AGO, SOME towns were looking for a name. So the town councils had all the townspeople come together and ask for suggestions. As it is normal, there were many, but most were not preferred for one or another reason. After a long day, the president of the council said,"Whatever suggestion comes up next, we will take it. I'm tired."

A new immigrant woman was sitting in the third row. Someone in the row behind her tapped on her shoulder. She turned around and, in broken English, demanded, "Who poken?"

"OK!" the council president declared, "Good enough! From now on, this town will be called Hoboken."

Another town had trouble; people brought others in from neighboring towns in to have a greater vote count for their choice of name, which made the council angry. So the president said,"The next time, no out-of-town people please—only those from our town should come—and alone." The citizens accepted this. The secretary, not too skilled, thought this was the name for the town, and wrote *Come* but accidentally added a stroke to the three that made up the "m", turning it into an "nn", and she put the "e" where the "a" had been in "alone".

And so Kinnelon was created.

At the meeting for a name in another nameless town, nobody could agree either. The meeting went on and on till night. Everybody got enormously tired, and one of the council members had to yawn. He opened his mouth wide, and out came something sounding like,"Mauhhhhwahhh."

Would you believe it? This is how Mahwah got to be named!

Matters got very ear-splittingly noisy at yet another town meeting. Because there was such a racket, the top guy at that meeting hollered,"Quiet, you bunch!What do you think? All we have to say, like a magician,"Hokus-pokus," and we have a name for the town?"There it was! Hokus-pokus sounded so good to everybody! But when they tried to write it out, they ran out of ink after Hokus and couldn't get to the Pokus. But then something seemed to be missing, and to make it look better, they stuck in another 'Ho,' and the town became known as Ho-ho-kus.

Two guys from different places tried to figure out what to call their towns. Each tried to help the other. . .so how to go about it? One said, "What's remarkable about your town?"

"Well, we have a lot of woods, with ridges in between—and yours?"

"We have a lot of stones."

"OK," the stone guy said. "Why don't you call your

town 'Ridgewood'?"

This sounded good to the wood guy, who replied, "We'll do that. From now on, we'll call our place 'Ridgewood'. But you have stones—what's the point there?"

"You're right," the stone guy said. "We have stones, and what's the point? Just a stony point."

"There you go!"

"Hey!" the stone guy said. "You're right. I have to thank you. From now on, we'll call our town 'Stony Point'."

And so two names for two towns were created. Was this not very neighborly?

Then there was a big farm with all kinds of animals and a shepherd, and a little boy who always wanted to go see the sheep. One Sunday, his parents took him in a buggy on an outing to see them.

His mother pointed to one and said, "There's the ram. See the big horns? And there's another ram—see over there?"

This became a special treat for the boy, to see those big horns.

Many years later, when the farm was gone and the land got to be a town, a name had to be found for it.

The boy, now a man, was appointed to the committee to choose a name. There was all kinds of debate over all kinds of names for the town, and it made him think back to how much simpler it had been for him as a boy, when his mother took him to see the rams with the big horns. He just could hear her saying, "There's the ram—see?" He told the committee that story, and all agreed to call the town "Ramsee," but, to make it look a little more elegant, they changed the spelling to "Ramsey." If you went there today, you wouldn't see the rams anymore—they've been gone a long while now, though you could see a train—but I doubt they'll change the name to"Trainsee".

One more nameless village grew to the point when it was time to find a name for it. Folks saddled their horses and went to one of the farmers for a meeting.

It had been a very dry year, and one of the farmers had a hard time getting water up on a hill, so his farm was very dry. The closer folks got to the farm next to the river, where the meeting was going to be held, the lusher the land became, because of that river water.

At the meeting all kinds of names were discussed, but none could be found that would please everybody. So the talk turned to the draught, and the farmer in the hills complained the most. The farmer next to the river said, "I have nothing to complain about. Look at my land."

This really got the other farmer mad. "You see, you have the river watering your land. What do you want me to do, saddle the river on a horse and ride it up to my place to get some water?"

All had to laugh, and it became a joke:"Saddle the river," indeed! But, before the day was out, they had their town's name: "Saddle River."

What would you name your town if you had the chance?

HOW WAS THIS AGAIN?

MY DAUGHTER CAME TO see us and asked my wife to change a fifty-dollar bill. My wife could find only two tens in her pocketbook. So they came to me, but I had only two twenties.

I put the two twenties on the table, and my wife added one of her tens. My daughter handed my wife the fifty; my wife put the fifty in her pocketbook, handed me the other ten, and called it even between us.

(Are you also so smart? If not, did you learn something?)

Use my wife's logic: I give forty; she adds ten to make it fifty. My daughter exchanges the money with her and then I get the second ten my wife had before. This puts me out thirty dollars, which my wife is pocketing.

Hopefully, my daughter doesn't want another fifty, or maybe even a hundred, changed too soon again. If they make change too often, I'll wind up in the poorhouse!

I LOVE TO EAT BRAINS

M Y GRANDDAUGHTER CERRIE BOUGHT me a shirt with pictures on it. One had an "I" with a red heart that contained the word brain: I love brain. She knows I love to eat calf's brains.

Here's why.

I know, at my age, the brain gets smaller in my head, so I figure if I put some in my stomach, it will replace some of that lost material in the head. Don't worry, though— it will not make me go "Moo" like a cow. I know because, when I was a youngster and my mother cooked a chicken, I always wanted the head in the chicken soup for the brain in it, and that did not make me go *"Kaaa, ka-ka, kaaaa"* like chicken either.

Come to think of it, just before I met my wife, when she was still a girl, I guess I must have had a chicken soup with a rooster head in it full of brains that day to eat. She impressed me so much that I suddenly became a rooster, went *"Ki-ke-ryyyy-keeee,* do you want to marry me?"

Luckily, she had eaten a cooked chicken brain too, and replied, *"Kaaa, ka-ka-kaaaa!* Of course, *jaja, jaaaaa*—and this was fifty-eight years ago. *Wowww!*

Siegfried Bader

ICE SKATING

SOME TIME BACK, WHEN I retired, to stay somewhat in
shape, I started taking a walk at 8 o'clock in the
morning around the lake at the reservation in Mahwah.
The lake actually is a pond in the Bergen County Reservation, with probably a mile of shore line. On February
1, 1992, when I retired, the pond was covered with ice sufficiently thick to walk across. Did I try? No. If had
walked across, that would have shortened my walk. . .
OK, I admit I chickened out.

One day, though, I must admit my wife, Anna, and
two of my grandchildren, Mary Anna and Joseph, went
with me on my walk, and we did go out on the ice. I was
the first to venture forth, only about three or four feet.

Mary Anna, who was five years old and had no walking experience on ice, saw me and came running. Before
I could warn her, she was on the ice; her feet went forward, then to the rear, and sideways; so did her hands.
Her face turned into two large eyes. To my surprise,
though, she was able to avoid falling. If somebody thinks
it is impossible to freeze instantly, I can now vouch for the
possibility. Mary Anna froze solid instantly; not a muscle

was moving. An instant before, her eyes had been as big as pizzas; then they were gone somewhere into her head. Finally a faint peep came: "Grandpa, help me. . ."

Joseph, not quite two years old, had in the meantime stepped out on the ice too, and down he went. He tried real hard to get up—first, with his legs, to get a grip; when this did not work, with his hands, but that did not work either—he could not hoist himself up from his stomach. When Grandma tried to help, he refused to accept the assistance.

After lots of some swimming type of movement, grunting noises, and banging his hands and feet, he finally admitted defeat. After Grandma put him on his feet and he was again on solid ground, he announced, "I don't like ice!" and that was it —not even a horse would have been able to pull him out on the ice again.

IT'S A MAN'S WORLD—OR IS IT?

Wife on phone to the blonde secretary looking for her husband in his office: "Where is he? Is he out again with that black-haired floozy?"

The blonde secretary:

"Oh no he is out with a business associate, a man, for lunch. You don't have to worry about the black-headed floozy anymore. I used all my charm on him to convince him she is not good for him at all. . . . No, no, he dropped her for good."

Is this maybe the end of the blonde?

Half a year later, wife on phone to brunette secretary, looking for husband in his office: "Where is he? Is he out with that blonde floozy?"

The brunette: "Oh, no, he's out with his business associate, a man, for lunch! You don't have to worry about the blonde floozy. I put in many hours after work in to convince him she's not good for him at all. . . . No, no, he promised me he won't see her again."

End of the brunette?

Half a year past,

Wife on phone to red-headed secretary, looking for husband in his office: "Where is he? Is he out with that brunette floozy?"

The red-head:"Oh, no—he's out with his business associate, a man, for lunch. You don't have to worry!"

Is this the end of the redhead?

Now, what is the point of this story? I don't know. Maybe he should have hired a gray head? . . . But, come to think of it, these gray heads have lots more experience!

So, you can see it is not about hair color. Black, blonde, red, brunette, it's about the women.

Ah! I hear the women say,"What about the business associate, the man he goes out with?"

Well, men do have to have free time with other men to recuperate sometimes—don't they?

IT JUST HAPPENS—DON'T ASK WHY

STORIES LIKE THE FOLLOWING ones occur in daily life; they can be very funny at the moment and, at the next, forgotten.

But they happen, and I hope you like them.

Fast Aging: Just after we got up, my wife was standing in the kitchen by the stove, wondering what to make for breakfast. I said to her, "Please let me take a good look at you today." I looked all over her face and deep into her eyes. My request had caught her off guard, and I could see in her face that she expected something nice would follow. "What is it you want to see?" she asked me.

"Oh," I told her, "I want to see how you look today, because if I look tomorrow you will be a day older." Needless to say, she grabbed a dish-towel and chased me through the whole house.

The Solicitation: Don't you get annoyed by solicitation on the phone? Normally my wife or I try to decline as politely as possible. Sometimes it is not possible, and we get drawn into a discussion we don't care for, the only solution is to abruptly hang up. From time to time, we get a call from Sprint asking us to switch to them. We have AT&T as our long-distance telephone company. So the last time Sprint called, it went like this:

Me: "Hello."

The caller from Sprint: "May I speak to Mr. Bader?"

Me: "Speaking."

"This is Sprint calling. Mr. Bader, I wonder if you would be interested in blah-blah."

I recalled a TV commercial from the company in which a needle is falling next to the phone and the connection is so clear that you can hear it hitting the table through your phone. "Hold on, please," I said. "Could you repeat what you just said, and speak a little louder? I cannot understand a word, and the connection on the phone is very bad. What company are you calling from?"

A long pause then, from Sprint: "Oh, uh, I'll call you another time."

It was the first time a solicitor had ever hung up on me.

The High Cost Of Health: The other day my wife had a little mole surgically removed on her shoulder. The doctor sent it to a lab for a biopsy. Today, in the mail, the bill for the biopsy came. My wife kept grumbling about the high bill. "Such a little thing, and right away so much money," and on and on she went. To stop this, I asked her what the diagnosis had been. "Positive or negative?"

"It don't matter, positive or negative. . .either way, it's *-tive!*"

The High Cost Of Living Increase: My left leg has been hurting for a while, the grass cutting season is here, and I ask my grandson (who's thirteen) if he'll cut the grass once a week for me. I promise him $5.00 every time he cuts it. My wife is supervising, so when I give him the $5.00, I give to her a dollar for supervising, to his immense surprise (I cannot believe she's taken it, too). This works for two weeks. Then he suddenly balks, and he says to me, "I'm tired—not today," or he can't because he's otherwise occupied. So my granddaughter (she's sixteen) says she'll cut it for $5.00, which she also did twice. Then I discover that their aunt, my other daughter, lets my grandson cut her grass too—for $10.00. Oh, now I guess I get it. . . This is a high cost of living increase! So I promise him the $10.00, too. Then I hear him telling his sister, "This is my job." Today he cuts it. Looking for the money to pay him, I discover I only have a twenty in my pocket, so what to do? He doesn't know. I tell him, "I only have a twenty here. Go cut the grass again, and I'll give you the twenty."

Then, somewhat mysteriously, he comes up with a ten from his pocket: To cut my grass twice in one day would be a little too much.

Tests In School: I had to drive to the ATM to get some money, and my grandson came with me for the ride. To make some conversation, I asked him what he had learned in school that day. "Well, we had some tests," he said. I could hear the disgust in his voice.

"This school is wrong," I said. "They shouldn't give a test, but a taste of an ice-cream, and all of the students will like it and everybody will be there."

At the bank, he watched what I was doing. I was withdrawing a hundred dollars, and when five twenties came out of the machine, he said,"Hey, this is easy," and I guess he was thinking, Why take a test when you can get money so easily at the bank.

The Car Keys: As you most likely know, new cars now come with a key and a remote to unlock and lock the doors. I hope they come up with a remote soon to find the keys when my wife shouts,"Car keys, where are you?"and the key answers, "Over here."

My wife needs something like this desperately. There is a hook on the wall to hang them; it's just that they don't hang themselves up.

So they're on the counter, or table in the dining room, or in the bedroom, or even, when she comes home and it's urgent, somewhere in the bathroom on a shelf. Then, when it's time to get in the car, "Where are my keys? I put them over here, and they're not here now."(That's what she thinks; who knows where she put them?)

I found the keys the other day on the kitchen counter, right next to some peaches she had bought. On the peaches was this little sticker no bigger than a thumbnail with a number on it. I peeled two off and stuck on the key-remote where the "open" and the "lock"buttons are.

When my wife looked for her keys, she could not see the open or lock buttons, just those stickers. She shrieked, "Oh, my god! What happened to my key remote?" When she realized what it was, I landed in the dog house for quite a while.

The Shoe On The Other Foot: My wife picks up our granddaughter and grandson most of the time after school is over. The other day she was not home, and the phone rang. It was my granddaughter, who said, "Tell Grandma not to pick me up at 2:00 from school."

A little later, the phone rang again. It was her mother, Irene, calling from work. "Did Ma pick up Mary Anna?"

I told her that her mother wasn't home, but that this was no trouble—I said Mary Anna had called and did not want to be picked up at 2:00 PM.

"What?" my daughter exclaimed. "They had off school at 1:00, and I told her to come home. So where is she? Why is she not listening?"

Mary Anna is now sixteen, and I guess there will be a lot of wondering where she is from now on—just as my wife wondered where her daughter Irene was at times when she was sixteen. I think the wonder-years are starting for her, and the shoe is on the other foot. My wife says Irene is in her forties, and she still wonders sometimes where she is. Mary Anna showed up at my house shortly thereafter and said she had walked over from school. I made her call her mother, and the day was saved.

I HAVE A GOOD IDEA, BUT THEN I'VE GOT A WIFE, TOO

THE OTHER DAY, I was watching a quiz show on TV. This question came up: "In his later years, Beethoven went deaf and composed without hearing. And what happened to Wagner?" It turned out Wagner went blind and did some great work without seeing.

This gave me a great idea; I'm half-blind already, especially in one eye. My hearing is very bad, too. If I go blind and deaf in the future, I will have a double greatness (Beethoven–Wagner style). Who knows what masterpieces I will be able to compose then? All I need is to buy a piano and compose great music, which I won't be able to hear or see.

Then I realized a piano will be in the way when my wife is vacuuming the floor, and it will be too hard to push around to make room. So I decided I will buy a piccolo instead. When I told my wife this great idea she gave me a look that said it all. Now I wonder how many great ideas from a man get killed by that look from his wife.

BATMAN

TODAY I WOKE UP without too much pain in my left hip-joint and leg. I have a pinched nerve in my back, and this has given me great deal of pain in my hip going down my leg for a few months already. I most likely need a back operation, according to my doctor. My wife had gotten up before me and was out in the kitchen. When there's not too much pain, I try to be funny, so I got up, took the sheet off the bed, wrapped it around me like a cape, and ran out into the kitchen, hollering,"Batman, Batman is coming!" and flapped the ends of the sheet like wings. To my surprise, she even laughed. (This is a big accomplishment for me.) So I had the courage to be even funnier. I turned to spread the sheet wider. I guess I should not have turned so fast. "Oh, my hip! Oh, pain!"

As I hobbled back to the bedroom, my wife asked "What's the matter?" All I could do was flap the sheet ends up and down a little and holler, "Batman, Batman is leaving and going away again."

A LETTER FROM MY CAR INSURANCE COMPANY

Siegfried,

Happy birthday from your friends at Plymouth Rock! We want you to know that we really appreciate your business, and we want you to enjoy your special day. That's why we're reminding you about Get Home Safe, a free benefit to our personal auto insurance customers.

After celebrating your birthday, if you feel too tired to drive, have a little too much wine at dinner, or just don't feel safe to drive, you don't have to get behind the wheel. Your cab fare is on us.

We wish you a safe and happy birthday, and a great year ahead!

My reply:

Thank you for the birthday wish, and don't worry—I don't drink, and you will not have to increase my insurance.

LUKOIL GAS STATIONS

HOW DID WE GET to have Russians own the Lukoil gas stations? A few years ago the Russians found big oil fields in Russia and the big shots from the oil companies all had a meeting about what best to do with all their oil.

One man suggested we sell it to the U.S.A. With all the cars there, they would certainly buy. All agreed, but what was the best way to do it? Another said,"Buy an oil-producing outfit in the U.S.A., and then sell it. All agreed, so they bought Mobil.

Then what? One said, "We can't keep the name, How can we get them to buy our benzene (Russian for gas)? Americans call it something different.

A different man suggested, "It doesn't matter what we call it. We peddle it a little cheaper, and it will work. They see the pumps and the price. This will say everything. We'll be selling."

The poor chump! He was almost disowned by the rest of them. Cheaper? They screamed, "We're here to make money! Go away—we don't need you any more, you— you dumb ?&^%$#."(This was all said, of course, in Russian; regretfully I don't know how to translate

?&^%$#.) So Cheap was voted down, and this dumb ?&^%$# had to sit in a corner.

But there was still no name. Another then said, "We and the Americans know the word 'oil,' right?"

"Yeah," said the guy sitting next to him. "But you put oil in the engine but not in the tank. The car don't run on oil. How do we get them to see benzene?"

"Wait a minute," came the reply from across the conference table. "You said 'see.' What do they say if they want you to see?"

"It sounds like 'look.' Then let's call it Look, Oil.

All agreed. But there remained a difficulty. How would they spell "Look." "Simple," one of them declared. "L-U-K! An"L" is an"L", a "U" is a "U", and a "K" is a "K", right? LUK!"

And that was how it got to be Lukoil.

On the other hand, maybe they wanted to name it Lucky Oil and just misspelled the word.

I went on the Internet to find out, but I had no luck (or "luk")—they had no conception of it. If you know how the name Lukoil got chosen, tell me. It is so important to know.

A MAN IS COOKING

MY WIFE IS GOING to Atlantic City today with the retirees from our town. I declined because I was still distressed from losing money the last time. My wife recuperates from such effects quicker than I, so she is going again. This is not the first time she is going without me, but today there is a difference: She wants me to cook. "What's the big deal about that?" you ask? I don't know how to cook!

All I know is that food is bought. Then my wife takes it into her sanctuary, called the "kitchen". In there, the food goes into vessels called "pots" or "pans", which are set on an altar called the "stove", in which fires are ignited to appease the gods. Sometimes she looks in a witchcraft book called *The All-Purpose Cookbook*; that's when it gets real tricky. Finally, she has a magic wand called a "wooden spoon," used to do some tricks in the pots or pans on the food and—oh, you get the idea.

She gives me some instructions: "The chicken is in the refrigerator—" there's something to be said for potatoes and onions— "and then cook a chicken stew." I'm watching the morning news on TV and pay no attention. After she leaves, I wonder, What did she say?

It doesn't matter. I'll show her that I can cook, and so where is this cookbook?

It took me an hour to find it. When I looked at the contents, the first chapter was about "Entertaining". Good, maybe I can learn some new jokes, I thought, but there was also something about setting tables. Why that was supposed to be entertaining escaped me, so I skipped that chapter.

I got to the chapter on drinks; was more entertaining than the chapter "Entertaining," and it made me real thirsty, too. I finally came to "Poultry."

First, they try to tell me what country all the geese, ducks, and chicken come from originally, which is nonsense. I know that; they came from eggs. On the next page, I found a bit on how "Dressing A Bird" is done. But I want to cook a bird naked as is, I am thinking. I don't want to dress a bird. No help there; I'd had enough and closed the book.

Ok. What did my wife say? Make stew! I don't like stew; I like oven-fried chicken, so oven-fried it will be. I need a pan; while I was looking for the cookbook, I had seen one. Here is the pan. Now the chicken goes into the pan.

With this done, what next? "Oil," I say aloud, so the chicken will not stick to the pan. When I found the bottle, it was only half full, though. I guess it will be enough, and into the pan it goes. "Salt." Two large spoonfuls should be enough; we always can add some more when we eat. What else is missing? Oh, "Garlic,"I say. Where's is the garlic powder?

While I was looking for the garlic powder, I found the paprika. It said "hot paprika" on the jar, but I used it anyway. It made the chicken look so nice, so red. Then I found the garlic powder—a full 2.5-oz. jar. How much to use? Half a jar should just bring out the flavor, I figured. What else? Onions and potatoes, of course—how could I forget? Do I peel the potatoes before or after cooking? I wondered.

Peeling is probably easier after, I told myself, so six un-peeled potatoes go into the pan.

I peeled and cut the onions, assuming that four should be enough. Now I know how they make all the movie stars cry. They cut a bunch of onions, put them in a bag, and hang it around the neck of the star. This way the star can cry to his or her heart's content. I understand now why dishtowels are the size they are— "to dry your tears," that's why; any smaller size wouldn't do.

Finally, I had it all in the pan and in the oven. I did not turn the oven on, because the idea of a home-made apple pie came to me. I don't want to bore you with how I made it. Enough said that I went to the store, got some apples, raisins, and a pie crust, and made a pie. Then I put the pie in the oven on the grill, above the chicken, so the chicken and pie would be done together. This was economical, don't you agree? Then I turned the oven on.

The next question was, How much heat? Let's see: Chicken, potatoes, onions, and apple pie—quite a bit in the oven, so it would need heat for sure. The maximum on the dial was 550°F.; I figured, I'll use this for about two hours, and then I'll look.

In half an hour, I had cleaned up the kitchen utensils I'd used so far. I could hear the chicken cooking, and soon it smelled pretty good, too. I went to read my paper in the living room until the time came to look.

Fifteen minutes of paper-reading later, the smoke alarm in the kitchen went off. When I got there, black smoke was pouring out of the stove. Something had gone wrong in the oven. I certainly didn't think there should be so much black smoke coming from it. The kitchen started to get dark; I turned the oven off and opened the oven door. That was a big mistake: A genie of black smoke got free.

Jumping back did not help; the genie got me. All I could think of was, "This is because I forgot to use the magic wand." Maybe I should have whacked the chicken a couple times with the wooden spoon and mumbled, "Abracadabra," before it went into the oven.

When the smoke cleared, I could see the pie had somehow climbed out of its burned-up crust and leaked down on the chicken. The chicken was kind of shriveled up, and the potatoes . . .I don't want to talk about it and relive it again, it was just a mess.

I put on some fans, and opened the windows, to get

the smoke out of the house; then I buried the chicken, the pie, and the potatoes back at the end of my garden. After that, I bought a new chicken, potatoes, and onions, and stopped by at KFC for four pieces of chicken and some fries.

I put the fresh chicken in the refrigerator to replace the burned one, and set the potatoes and onions where they belonged. Then the clean-up of the kitchen started. I finished just a half hour before my wife got home.

When she entered the house, I asked how she had done. She said she had won fifty cents. "Oh, good," I said. "Now you have $40.50."

"No, I have fifty cents," she replied. "I left with $40.00. I lost $39.50. I could have lost all of it, but I did not lose the last fifty cents. I'm back with fifty cents, so I won fifty cents, you see?" I cannot beat this type of logic, so I kept my mouth shut.

"What did you cook?" she asked.

"KFC chicken," I told her.

"I thought you would make a stew," she said.

I had to think fast. "I went to work," I said.

"You went to work? You're retired, remember?" she shot back suspiciously.

"Oh, they needed me to do something only I could help with."

She went to the fridge, looked in, and said, "How come this chicken you were supposed to cook got so small?" Drats; I must have bought a smaller chicken than the one she had, and she'd noticed it. Think quickly, you old geezer.

"The frost-free cycle is going on too much in the fridge. It must have dehydrated the chicken. I'll have to check the fridge,"I said.

"I smell a rat in this answer, but I'm too worn out to ask for the right one,"she replied. Man, how lucky I'm that she's tired, I thought. For that I lit a candle.

The next day, as we were having breakfast, she looked out the kitchen window. "That darn dog again," she said.

"What are you talking about?" I asked.

"That big dog always runs through our garden and yard. I could have sworn this time he had a chicken in his mouth."

Oh, boy. I could smell a rat myself. I tried to sneak out the back way. "Where are you going?" she asked.

"To the garden, to look," I replied.

"Wait I'll come too," she said.

How could I stop her?

At that moment, the phone rang. This is what I call Saved By The Bell. For that, I lit two candles later at church.

When I got in the garden, sure enough the dog had dug out the chicken, and a flock of birds was gorging on the now-exposed pie and potatoes and onions. "Get the hell out of here, you, critters!" I barked. I had just enough time to bury it all again before my wife came out.

The next time, I'll go to Atlantic city, too. It's simpler.

MOTHER'S DAY

WILL WRITE THE following story as if it happened to me, although it is pure fiction—believe me. If the names in the story match those of my family members, this is utterly coincidental.

The Saturday before Mother's Day, my son and his family were invited to our house for dinner because they were going somewhere else the following day. Christina, my middle daughter, had volunteered to cook, so my wife, a granddaughter, Cerrie, and I could go to the Ramapo Valley Reservation. There we met my son Michael, his wife Rona, and their two sons, Justin and Drew, for a walk before we went to our house to eat.

I went shopping Friday but forgot to get a Mother's Day card for my wife. No problem, I'll get it Saturday, I thought. Saturday morning, I got busy doing something, and then it was time to meet my son at the reservation and I had no card. I finagled my wife and Cerrie out into the car to be able to ask Christina to get one for me. As I was handing a $5.00 bill to Christina, my wife came back in the house again, so I whispered, "Get a card—I need one for Mom."

Christina nodded, and everything was dandy.

The walk, the dinner, and the rest of the day were all fine. I had no way to ask Christina where the card was. She'd had to go to work before everybody left. When I looked for the card, I could not find it. As soon as she gets home from work tomorrow, I told myself, I have to find out where it is.

On Mother's Day, my wife was up early, Christina wasn't home yet, and I had no card, so I pretended I was still sleeping.

Finally, Christina walked in, and I murmured,"Where did you put it?"

"In the refrigerator! Where else would you put it?"

"What?"

At that moment, I realized, What a trick! Where did old men, when I was young, hide money from their wives? In the torn sock drawer, of course, where the wives never looked. The refrigerator, of course! My wife would not cook that day, so she would not look there. What logic my daughter had shown, thinking just as I would have.

After I emptied half the refrigerator and still found no card, however, my wife came into the kitchen. "Oh, my god—what are you doing?"

"Uh, defrosting the refrigerator," I said.

"Do you do this very often? On a frost-free unit? And always on a Sunday?" she asked.

"Oh, no" I replied. "Only when the Sunday is a Mother's Day. . . . You're right, though. I'll put everything back."

She shook her head as she left, and I replaced every-thing in the fridge.

After that, I went to my daughter and whispered, "Now, tell me—where's the card?"

"What card?"she wanted to know.

"The card you were supposed to get with the five dol-lars I gave you!"

She stared at me. "You asked for some codfish, and it's in the refrigerator."

Slowly it dawned upon me that there had been a mis-understanding.

"I told you to get me a card, for Mom," I said.

"No, you told me get some cod for Mom. I know she doesn't like codfish, though, so it kind of surprised me."

So I'd gotten codfish for Mother's Day, and my wife nothing. As I looked out the window, wondering what she would say if I handed her the codfish, I spotted some beautiful flowers right near the fence—long-stemmed and bright yellow, with lush green leaves. And I remembered how, a long time ago, as a little boy, I had picked dande-lions for my mother for Mother's Day, and she had said, "This is the best gift I ever got!"

Out I went, picked the most beautiful dandelions I could find, put a rubber band around them, went to my wife, said, "Happy Mother's Day," and handed her the dandelion bouquet.

At first I could see puzzlement, followed by a touch of anger turning to softness and understanding in her eyes.

The dandelions where gracefully accepted and put in a vase.

Mothers do not change at all over the years—when a little boy comes and brings a gift, whether he's a son of six or a husband of sixty. All mothers, I'm sure, will understand what I mean.

And with this, my pure fiction ends.

A happy mother's day to all mothers—especially my mother and my wife. For them it goes double.

Siegfried Bader

MOWING THE LAWN

YESTERDAY MORNING, BEFORE SHE left the house to go babysitting my grandchildren, my wife asked me to mow our neighbor's lawn.

"What's the matter with it? Why should I cut it?" I asked, taken by surprise. "I'll disturb her."

"You won't disturb her," she assured me. "She left for two days to visit a friend, and the man who's supposed to mow it hasn't shown up for two weeks now. She did me a favor, so I volunteered you to return it."

While I was working with all this overtime at my job, I have to admit I never mowed the grass at home. My wife did it, or my son or daughter. Actually, I dislike gardening, cutting grass, or trimming bushes and shrubs. My wife has the green thumb, so stuff like that has always been her domain. She knows the names of all the green things. I only know that, when something grows in the garden, it's for eating. When something grows on the lawn, it's grass. Bushes and flowers bloom and make you sneeze. Lawn, garden, bushes—for me, they're all unimportant things.

I do know about more important things, like, for example, the fact that the Milky Way is not a way where the cows give milk to the farmer, but our galaxy, and that it's got a diameter of hundreds of thousands light years (which is much longer than the preceding sentence). Or that the nearest star is four and a half light years away.

My wife, on the other hand, only figures distances by how far a dollar's worth of gas gets her. I'd like to see if she can figure out what it would cost to get to the nearest star.

Since I retired and my wife started babysitting, I took over mowing the grass, like it or not. Our lawn is done in about a half hour; our neighbor, a widow, has the same size property. I assumed that it should take just about as long, and went to take a look. I found that she has no storage shed; we do. We store wood for burning in the winter, and the shed covers a lot of grass. She doesn't. Plus, we have an above-ground swimming pool for the grandchildren, and a garden. So, altogether, she has at least three times as much grass to cut as I. The property certainly looks much bigger. How did I get into this? I asked myself.

I remembered saying something in my vows about health and till death. . .but I didn't remember anything about having to make good on a promise my wife made to a neighbor. On the other hand, so much time has passed since the day we married, I told myself, maybe I did. In any case if I didn't cut the grass, my wife would be in a bad mood that would turn into a migraine. I figured I'd better do it.

I was sure the man who was supposed to come and

cut the grass had not come for four weeks, because it was ten inches high. She had several flowering trees in the front yard, and, surrounding them, I could see a spot five feet in diameter where no grass should be. Even so, there was a big-leaf type of grass already growing there.

It took two hours to cut the lawn. I had an especially hard time around the trees because the branches were so low. I could understand why a zone free of grass around the trees was necessary. Twice I had to fill the gas tank on my mower to get all the grass cut, but when I was done I was proud of myself and took a deserved rest.

In the evening, when my wife came home, her first question was, "Did you cut the lawn?"

I played innocent. "What lawn?"

"The neighbor's," she replied, and, in a harsher voice, "I asked you this morning to—"

"Gosh darn it, I knew you told me something, but I could not remember what."

She stared at me. "Stop fooling around. I'd better take a look."

When she had left, I waited in anticipation for the pat on my shoulder and the praise I would get.

In three minutes my wife was back. "What did you do to the phlox under the trees? You cut it all off. How could you do that?"

I could see the pat and the praise waving good-bye. "What phlox under the trees?" I asked. "Don't tell me that stuff under the trees was not grass."

"No! It was phlox," she said.

"I told you not to tell me that."

"Stop this Maxwell Smart thing! You see I'm not laughing."

For the rest of the day my wife had a headache. I could not win; whether I cut or did not cut the grass, she had a headache.

This morning I bought fifty dollars' worth of phlox and planted them under the trees. They look good, too—if you did not know, just as if it were the original ones.

When the neighbor came home a little while ago, she dropped by and thanked me for cutting her grass.

"Oh, it's OK," I said. "You're welcome."

"I noticed," she continued, "that you watered the phlox around the tree and loosened all the dirt up, but if you cut the grass next time, just cut the phlox too—I don't want it anymore. I'd like to plant lilies."

I was speechless for a few seconds. By the time I got control over my body back, I was ready to choke somebody. Luckily, my wife stepped behind my chair, grabbed me by the shoulders, and pushed me down.

"OK," she said, "he'll do that next week."

That's what they think; I cannot afford to cut her lawn again, I'll go broke.

By this time next week, I'll be in Alaska. There the summer is much shorter. Less grass to cut.

MUSIC OF ICE

OVERNIGHT THE TEMPERATURE WENT down to the single digits, and I wondered if I should go for my walk; by the time I made up my mind, an hour had passed. Most mornings, there is nobody walking but me, and I enjoy the fresh air and the quiet. This morning, the sun was shining on the frozen lake, and the temperature in the Mahwah Reservation was rising fast.

As I walked, I noticed something disturbing the silence; I could not make out what it was—a distant jet or the wind in the trees. The sound was almost as if people were swinging ropes or sticks through the air. As I neared the lake, I suddenly realized the sun was warming the surface of the ice. Tension was building up between the warmer surface and colder interior.

Within a few minutes, all kinds of noises traveled across the ice. You could hear whistles moving from shore to shore with the speed of a bullet, knocking from the top or the bottom, at times as soft as a pebble would sound when it falls, at times like a sledgehammer swung by ghostly hands. Murmurs of a women's voice changing to a man's also appeared, just not understandable.

There were hundreds of sounds at the same time. This was all so incredibly beautiful—like a laser light show in sounds.

Fifteen minutes later, it was all over. When I left an hour later, there were still some noises, but not the "show." If I had taken my walk at my usual time, I would have missed something that I have never heard in my sixty years and most likely will not hear again.

My wife and I went another day; there was some activity on the ice, but it was not the same. The night was milder, and it was probably not the right temperature during the day. Besides, when I took a closer look at the ice, I could see hundreds of cracks running through it. Maybe that silenced the sound, too.

MY DAUGHTER DRIVING

NOWADAYS WHEN I GO shopping and I have one of my children or grandchildren with me, I let them do the driving—after all, I want to enjoy what's going on outside looking out the window. Too many times I hear, "Did you see that beautiful house?" or "Ha! Look how many birds there are sitting on that electrical wire!" or "Whoa—just look how many geese there are over there," or "Oh, somebody must have hit this tree!" I'm driving, and I have to miss this all because I have to keep my eyes on the road to see if a dog or cat might cross it."

So when my daughter went shopping with my wife and me the other day, I went outside while they were still a little behind me in the house, started the car, backed it out of the carport, got out, and handed the keys to my daughter—not because I want to be able to have more time to sight-see, oh, no. Keep on reading, and you'll find out why.

"What, I have to drive?" she asked.

"Sure. I'll let you and Mom sit in the front."

I did not want to tell her that, with one of them in the back, they just talk, one bent forward and talking right over the front seat-back and into my ear enough for it to go numb. With both of them in the front seats, I can pretend I'm sleeping or shut my ears, depending on what is being said. My wife can certainly talk while we drive regardless of how far we go—never tired, and never at a loss for words. . . .

Not that I complain—far from it, believe me—because sometimes I hear things I never would hear any other way. But in general, it's pretty ho-hum stuff. Just don't tell them; otherwise, they might shut up, and I'm won't be informed about what happens around me anymore, and this would be a real shame, you know? I and uninformed would be like a. . .a. . .well, you give it a name, and that's what I would be! They haven't told me yet what to call it.

Now, is this not a revelation to myself? How proud I am. I guess I'd better keep listening to them to be informed and not miss anything.

If you let somebody else drive and not you, you're not always hugging that steering wheel, and you might even pick up some illuminating insights into yourself. So good luck to you, too. Maybe you will also have to write about something interesting sometime.

MY FAMILY TREE

I ASK MYSELF WHOM I most resemble on my family tree. So I start climbing it, and browsing from branch to branch: this branch, no; that one, no way. . .and, finally, there it was. So I slithered down the branch to where I should be now.

Aha! This is me, and I discover that this branch so full of worms in my life, and the woodpecker called Time has pecked so many holes in it, that, at the age it is by now, it's ready to break off and be gone.

End of my story.

MY GEESE ENCOUNTER

TODAY WHILE I TOOK my daily walk around the lake, I had an encounter with two wild geese. I walked near the water, and about sixty to eighty feet ahead of me. . .

Let's go back a little to explain.

Oh, OK, the geese—what about the geese!

Today I walked along the shore of the lower lake in the Mahwah Reservation. It's winter, but the last few days have been nice, and the ice is completely gone. About eighty feet ahead and about sixty feet to the right, there was a little rise in the ground. Two geese came walking over from the lake. I did not see them, nor did they see me, until they were on top of the rise. There was a smaller goose, which I assumed was the female, and a larger one, the male, and the surprise between them and me was mutual.

Both let out a scream. If somebody had been dead and buried here, I'm sure they'd have awakened, thinking some angel was blowing the trumpet to announce the end of the world and the advent of the Resurrection.

She shut up fast, though, and, with a long stride, waddled to the water. He didn't. He thrust his head forward, spread his wings, and started more or less marching in my direction, hissing.

Now, wait a minute—what do I have here? An attack goose, like the attack rabbit our former president Carter had?

Carter, if you remember, was attacked by a rabbit swimming in the water of some lake while he was fishing in a boat. He at least had a paddle to defend himself, but I was not much larger than that goose. On the other hand, he was hollering all kinds of geese curses at me. I'm sure even an army sergeant would have learned something new if it had been comprehensible.

So I did what any hero would do: I opened my coat and spread it apart with my hands. I must have look like a bird with some enormous wings to him, because he fled like oiled lightning into the water. They hollered a couple more curses at me from their safe distance in the water, turned around, quacked something else, and swam off.

I looked over my shoulder to the right, then the left. There was nobody around. Good. I shouted my best Tarzan shout for victory. Let the geese wonder too what I said to them.

That should have been the end of the story, but no sooner had the last echo of my Tarzan yell faded in the distance, and then, from across the lake, a man I had not seen yelled back, "Hey, you showed *them*, didn't you!" Needless to say, my walk was very short today. I certainly did not look for the guy, because I preferred not to encounter him.

MY DAILY MEDICATION ROUTINE!

S INCE I HAVE REACHED the ripe old age of eighteen—gee, oh no, I mistyped that, you know, my fingers have arteritis, or is it spelled *arthritis*? They do stuff with me I'm telling you, and I wanted to type eighty-one, not eighteen, and when you're my age you'll understand what fingers can do without you knowing anything about it. So now you know, I have to take some medication to get to be eighty-two (or is it twenty-eight?).

The names of the medications have some kind of badly misspelled English meanings, you know. They are spelled Aggrenox, Amlodipine, Bystolic, Donepezil, Glyburide, Metformin, Lisinopril, and Zetia. They fill my stomach, and for what? So I stay skinny, of course; that is what my doctor wants.

Translations: Look closely what they truly want to spell

"Aggrenox": To get "not angry"

"Amlodipine": "Almost be mine" (but she is my wife already)

"Bystolic": "Store it", or "a pistol"

"Donepezil": "Take a pencil"

"Glyburide": "Get lost / Take a ride"

"Metformin": "I mean it "

"Lisinopril": "Bawling"

"Zetia": "That is an ultimatum"

So every day, when I have to take the pills—but then, where are they? I have to look for them, you know (it is age related; at this age you put something somewhere the day before . . . but where?)—the whole process makes me so "Aggrenox" that I called "Amlodipine" to ask, "Where did you 'Bystolic?' my medication again?" She "Lisinopril" at me. "I really 'Metformin' it. Why don't you 'Donepezil' and write it down, so you don't always have to ask me what you did with it? Change your routine, or I will 'Glyburide' out the door, and that is the last 'Zetia' you see of me. Do you understand?"

When she was last Lisinoprilling at me, her voice was so angry and so loud that it was thundering, and when it thunders, I hide under the bed.

And lo and behold, that's where my medication was.

I came out from under the bed with the medication and told "Amlodipine", "Please don't be 'Aggrenox' at me, and do not 'Lisinopril' anymore. I found it."

"Good," she said. "Now that you've found it, eat your breakfast, take those pills and 'Glyburide' into the other room, and don't make me 'Aggrenox' again—I might use a 'Bystolic,' and then you won't get to be eighty-two."

This is, when you get old, kind of a daily routine. So I ask myself, do I really want to get to maybe be ninety, and have even more medications with bad English names to write about? Let me sleep on this before I answer it.

Now, don't be Aggrenox—I promise, I will tell you all about it sometime before I am ninety.

MY NAME IS FRED, OR IS IT?

Wʜᴇɴ I ᴡᴀs ʙᴏʀɴ in 1931, I was christened "Siegfried" Bader. Siegfried is a name out of the old Germanic mythology. I used it until I immigrated to the United States in 1956.

When I started work at Mr. Lott's garage in Jeffersonville, New York, my boss had some trouble pronouncing "Siegfried." Every time he called me to do something, I did not react quickly enough. He asked me how to pronounce my name, and I told him. When he repeated it, it came out entirely different and sounded very English to me; my English was really poor then, so I stopped paying attention.

This went on for a few days before he'd had enough and said, "I call you and call you, and you don't listen. What you want me to call you?"

I did not know and shrugged.

"You know, you have something like 'fried' in your name. You're in the States now, and 'Siegfried' is pretty uncommon. I'm going to call you 'Fred' from now on."

So everybody over here calls me Fred.

I didn't tell this to the authorities here; they still think I'm Siegfried, and my legal signature is still Siegfried Bader, and that is all, and it will stay this way.

But to you I'm Fred. Unless you want to call me Siegfried.

MY SISTER THE ACROBAT

WHEN WE WERE TEENAGERS, my sister could stand on her head much better than me—it did not matter how I tried, period. I know you're thinking that was because I was holding her feet to balance her. Oh no, I didn't do that; it was not necessary. Just the opposite. I sometimes tried to push her over, not hold her; she was just better than me. But I had something to do with it anyhow. It was not all her doing, at least I don't think it was. . . .

How come, you would like to know?

When she was a few months old, I was playing in the yard. My mother came out with her in the baby carriage, pushing her around to get her to go to sleep. I don't remember, of course, whether she did this to me, too.

I was hanging on to the carriage at the other end, where my sister's head was. "Don't do that!" my mother said. "You'll tip the carriage over."

But walking next to the carriage with my mother pushing it was too slow for me, so I ran around it, and her, several times while she moved along, but I was still touching the carriage here and there.

We passed a little flower bed, and my mother let go of

the carriage and bent down to do something with the flowers. I was at that moment again at the head end of the carriage and, since I was standing there, I hung onto it. But, since the counterbalance of my mother was no longer there, in the next moment the carriage flipped over, and I was on the ground, and my baby sister, in the carriage, was standing on her head.

"Oh, my god!" my mother screamed. "I told you so many times not to hang on to the carriages like this." My sister yelled too, I guess at me—I don't know what she said because I had forgotten all my baby talk by then, so I did not understand her and can't say for sure what she was shrieking.

So I ran away as fast as I could.

Luckily, she was OK, and, when I had the courage to go home, the lecture I got from my mother was not too bad, considering I'd heard it all before.

So I got her to stand on her head as a baby a couple months old, so she had to be better than me at it. Nobody ever made me stand on my head that early in my life.

I still feel appalled that I was not a helpful big Brother to her.

I should have been better and apologized instead of running away.

But since she has grown to adulthood with this fine skill, I realize I have nothing to apologize for, and I feel better already!

MY SISTER THE DEMANDER

WHEN MY SISTER WAS born, I was about five years old, and the excitement in the family was great. She got what she wanted, and she always wanted what I had in my hand. If I did not hand it over, you should have heard her: She was able to make a big spectacle of it.

So my mother always said to me in German, "*Gibs ihr schon endlich,*"("Give it to her already"), and I did, because I was always told, "You are the big brother, and she is a girl—you have to be gallant!"

My sister caught on fast. After "Mama" and "Dada," her third words were"*Gibs ihr*" ("Give her"). I lost some of my toys this way because, if she got one, I got it back-broken.

When I did get a present for any occasion, I always asked for comic magazines. They were, in Yugoslavia, mostly in the Serbian language. Although I am German, I was able to speak and understand all spoken Serbian, and read some too really well by seeing what was happening in the pictures. There were Krnjo, similar to Denis the Menace; Mandrakes, like The Phantom; and my favorite, the tree Urgususy. This was something about three men. One had a very big beard on his face, the second one eye patched up, and the third a really large nose. They got into all kinds of trouble, like the Three Stooges over here.

At Christmas, when I was seven or eight years old, I got the three Urgususy—the whole year of this magazine—put into a book as a present. This book was kind of a treasure to me, and hid it from my sister till she caught me.

She wanted it too, and screams of "*Gibs ihr*" followed until my mother told me to give it to her for a little while. I did not want to, but Mother said so, I had to. I handed it to my sister and walked away.

An hour or so later I wanted my book back and went to get it.

There was my sister with the book. She had ripped pages out it, and they were lying all around her on the floor. I shrieked and tore the book out of her hands. She yelled, "*Gibs ihr!*" demanding it back. I had just raised the book high, not to prevent her from reaching it but to hit her over the head with it, when my mother suddenly appeared, grabbed the book from behind of me, and shouted, "What is going on?"

I did not have to explain; she saw it all.

To my surprise, she screamed at my sister, who became speechless and noiseless so fast it came as quite a surprise to my mother and me both.

But my book! I put the pages back as well as I could, but it was gone anyway.

But from that moment on, I no longer had to hear

"*Gibs ihr*" about anything any more.

Epilogue: Yes there were moments we were angry at at each other. We live now, with our families, halfway around the world, and are much older, but she is still my sister and I will always be her brother, and we will have our love for each other for the rest of our lives.

MY WIFE IS SOLVING ALL

YESTERDAY I HAD TO reconcile my bank account on my computer in Quicken, and I somehow found a mistake for the second time—not big but still there. After the first time, I'd made sure it was right before closing, but this time, there it was one again.

I couldn't understand it. Was my program being attacked by an invader testing me to see if I noticed it, and who knew if it would be worse in the future? It was upsetting me, and I figured I would change my password in Quicken.

But this not so easy to do—first to find out how, then to get a good word (this is easily done, but I have to remember it too when needed, which is not so easy). I had done stuff like that, written down a password, but then where did I put this note? Definitely not where I remembered I had!

My anger grew, and I complained to my wife and said,"I think I will have to change my password. I just don't know to do it so it's secure and I can remember it."

She looked at me. "That's easy. Change it to 'Wilee-waleewo-wiliwaliwaliwo'. This is just like one-two-three, and nobody will ever be able to break it again.

Was this not easy? It is, always. From now, on I say to my wife, "Password, please," and I'm in my program. Good to have a wife to help out—don't you agree?

(Just one problem: she or I have to always spell it right, and hopefully she is not in the supermarket when I need the password.)

NO HELP IN THE STORES

THE OTHER DAY, MY wife sends me to buy some chicken in the grocery store. I see some chickens selling for $1.19 a pound. The chicken legs cost only $1.59 a pound. The wings cost only $1.59 a pound. But then boneless chicken breast cost $1.79 a pound, twenty more cents than the chicken legs with the bones still in them. At 60 cents a pound, I can get a complete chicken, which gives leftover bones for to make the cat happy.

I'm thinking that the meat with bones in it is cheaper. It makes sense, because you cannot eat the bones, so it costs less. But a chicken breast has no bones; that make sense too, but that costs more.

Then I have an idea. I look around. Maybe I can find something between $1.79 and $1.59 a pound, but I can't. So I go to the butcher counter and ask (it can't hurt, can it?).

I tell the butcher that all I see is boneless chicken breast for $1.79, which costs more than the $1.59 or than the rest of the chicken meat with bones. "Since manly breasts are less meaty," I tell him, "do you have any? And how much would a boneless rooster chest cost?"

He could not even speak; all he could do slap his forehead with his hand.

I was not sure—had I given him a hot new selling idea?

He said, "Hah? I don't understand?"

"Well, a boneless rooster chest must be scrawnier than a chicken breast, no? And shouldn't that be cheaper? I think so. Don't you too?"

He just walked away.

The help you get nowadays in the stores is terrible.

Maybe he doesn't understand English.

NOTHING IS THE SAME ANYMORE

A S IT SNOWS TODAY and I look out the window, I start to remember that, when we were substantially younger, the snow was fun. Especially when we, that is my wife Anna and I, and sometimes my neighbor Henry Baker and his wife Nancy, went sled riding.

There's a nice hilly road in my neighborhood on Church Street, in Mahwah, that comes down in a straight line and is right for sled-riding. We spent many hours after work with sleds, walking up the road and shushing down again on the sled, and again, without getting tired of it.

Then, there were fewer homes around here, and the traffic was very light. But nowadays all is built up, and there are too many houses, and too many cars. Times have changed, the neighborhood has changed, Henry moved to another house in town a long time ago, and the winters have changed as well. There's less snow now, and the less snow I see, the better I like it. Now it's a nuisance to me.

One afternoon back then, my wife and I went for a sled ride. Henry joined us. My wife did not want to go first, but I promised I would push her to the beginning of the hill so she didn't have to walk. All she had to do was kneel on the sled, and I put my hand on her back and pushed her. This was fun, and off we went. When Henry joined me in pushing, we made a pretty good headway to the hill.

On the way up the road, we decided that my wife could go on the sled for the first run all by herself. Soon we reached the top of hill; one more hard push, and she would be on her way down. There was just one problem—it was getting dark, and we did not realize that the sand truck had showed up before us. So when I gave her the final push, the sled came to a sudden stop a little farther down the hill, stuck in the sand.

My wife, still kneeling on the sled, was suddenly off balance and leaned forward. The sled, because of the curve in the runners, like on a rocking chair, tipped slowly with the front end getting lower and lower. In slow motion, she and the sled tipped further and further forward. Her behind, and the rear end of the sled, were suddenly so high that she slid off with her nose and face into the road: Kaboom! There she was, still half on the sled and half with her head on the road, in the snow, screaming something I could not understand, whatever it was. I think was better that I didn't.

After I rescued her from this position, Henry and I had to laugh so hard we almost dropped into the snow ourselves. It was not so much fun for my wife, though; while she was rubbing her face, and especially her nose, she let me know what an "Idiot!"I was. As if it was my fault that the road had been sanded and the sled stopped suddenly. Or as if it was my fault that she wanted to go down the hill kneeling on the sled all by herself and not sitting. And for sure I had not put the curve on the runner of the sled!

To this day, after forty-plus years, whenever Henry sees my wife, he asks her if she'd like to go for a sled ride. Times maybe have changed, but some things will not be forgotten and stay the same, and when my wife is angry at me over something, I do hear about this mishap yet again.

OH IT'S SNOWING!

I look out the window, and what do I see?
Oh, how busy I will be.
Silent is the falling snow.
I wish away that it would go.
Please don't let it get a hold. . . .
Because it makes me feel so cold.

Silently is the falling snow.
Santa Claus, with a Ho, ho, ho
He did bring me a shovel for Christmas,
And out the window, what a stress!
Out there, such a snowy mess!
I have to go out and use this shovel
Now, I guess?

OH, WHAT A BEAUTIFUL GIRL SHE IS

T O UNDERSTAND THIS BETTER: We lived in Yugoslavia at that time, and most people spoke a number of languages because of border changes from Austria/Hungary to Yugoslavia. This created multiple nationalities in the land. For example, my father knew four: our own language was German, and then he spoke Serbian, Hungarian and Romanian. My mother was familiar with three: German, then Serbian, and Hungarian. I, at that time, knew three: very good German, Serbian, and some Hungarian. Later on, I learned English.

When I was about five, my mother and I sometimes went for a walk. There was another woman, with a little girl of around three, taking a walk, too. My mother stopped to talk with her many times. They were Hungarian, and the little girl's name was Piroshka ("Rosie" in English). The conversation was always in Hungarian, because the other woman did not know German. My understanding of Hungarian was not too great then, but I could talk some to Piroshka about whatever children talked, and she understood me.

After they left, my mother always gushed in German

to me about how beautiful Piroshka was: "Did you see the beautiful eyes she has, and the dark long hair?" and so forth. Of course, I agreed with her, and I was taken, too (you say I was too young, but I did not think so; she was beautiful).

One day, I was all by myself, coming home from somewhere, and there was Piroshka all by herself on the street, standing a few houses away from where she lived. What is she doing over here alone? I wondered. She must be lost, this poor beautiful little girl. I'd better help her to get home again. So, really eager and with the knowledge of the older person I was in my mind, I approached her and told her (in Hungarian), "I will bring you home."

All she said was, "Nemm" (which means "no" in Hungarian), so I tried to take her hand to walk her home, but she would not let me do it. Now what is this? I asked myself. Here I am, gallantly showing her how much I care for her, and a "nemm"is her answer?

I had to do what my mother did to me. If I didn't do what she wanted me to, she'd take me by the hand whether I liked it or not and make me do it. But when I tried to grab Piroshka's hand, wham! I got my first-ever slap in my face.

It was my first slap, and my first rejection of a "beautiful" girl I admired, liked, even loved, and I was just trying to be gallant and bring her home safely! What a letdown! I went crying to my mother and told her what that "repulsive" girl had done to me. I told her, "This I will never forget!"

That was almost eighty years ago, but as you can see, I do still remember it, have kept my promise to never forget.

And no girl has ever had to slap me since! At least my beautiful wife hasn't, although sometime she asks, when she doesn't like something I'm doing, "Do you want a kick in your pants?"(But she only asks—and if she did kick me, I don't know whom I'd run to now to cry!)

I have no idea what happened to Piroshka after that, nor do I recall whether my mother ever claimed she was such a beautiful girl after that. I have forgotten my Serbian and Hungarian as well, because too many years have passed since I spoke either of them.

But "Piroshka," as you see, I do still remember is "Rosie" in Hungarian.

PERFORMING GOOD DEEDS

MY WIFE WAS IN the Good Samaritan Hospital in Suffern, New York, in 1959. In the same room was an older lady with her own complaints. Since we had only been in the United States for three years at that time, my wife's English was not very good, so the woman felt sorry for her. When the doctor told my wife she was pregnant and left, the woman said, "Don't worry—I will help you always."

Our son Michael was born in February 1960, and the woman was really helpful to us, so a long friendship with her and her husband started that lasted for their lifetimes.

Molly was like a mother to my wife. Her husband's name was Nelson. They had a son, Russell, and lived in Waldwick, New Jersey. They had an old Chevrolet.

I know you want to hear about my good deeds, not somebody else's. By then, I had bought our house in Mahwah. Nelson's car had engine trouble in 1968. Since I had worked all my grownup life on cars, and had already been with the Ford assembly plant in Mahwah for ten years, I knew an engine bearing was causing Nelson's problem. He was very upset because he was retired and his son was in college, so did not have the money to buy a new car, and the garage's repair estimate was very high. So I said I'd help him if I could.

I had most of the hand tools for car repair, and at that time you could order bearings from the automobile parts store in Suffern. I also found out I'd be able to pick up all of the special tools I'd need from a tool rental place.

I was due for a vacation and took a week off. With Nelson's car in my driveway, I jacked it up, put it on cinder blocks, crawled under it, took the oil pan off, and changed the bearings. My father-in-law, who was visiting us from Salzburg, Austria, at that time, helped me lift and hold the oil pan up so I could bolt it back up again. The car ran perfectly when I was done, and Nelson only had to pay for the new bearings, since I took care of the tool rental myself.

Nelson and I had many great times until his lung cancer was discovered a few years later. My wife and I helped them many more times, especially when he was very ill, to get to all the doctors' appointments. Their son had married and had moved Cape May Court House in South Jersey, and it was not possible for him to help too much.

Six years after Nelson's death in 1972, we took Molly with us for a visit to see my mother in Austria for a month. Molly knew her very well by then, since my mother had come to visit us in Mahwah many times. After we were back, Molly said it was the best vacation she'd ever had.

Eventually Molly moved to South Jersey, where her

son was a school principal and wound up in a nursing home. The last time we saw her alive, she recognized my wife but not me anymore. We still remember Molly and Nelson very much.

I know enough is enough of bragging about good deeds I have done, but my daughter insists I mention another one since she was there and it impresses her, describe what a good thing I did (I'm lucky she doesn't know all of them, or I'd never be done writing).

All six of us were shopping in the Alexander store in Paramus. We went browsing around. There was some display the children wanted to see before we left the store. It was close to the checkout lines, and in one of the lines, a woman was waiting to checkout with her pocketbook hanging wide open over her shoulder. A man came up behind her and slid his hand into it! Instantly, I knew he was stealing, but the woman did not know or feel it. Before I could get there, a store guard came running and the women started screaming. By then, the man had his hand, with the wallet, in his pocket.

People standing in the lines broke up and were running in all directions. Somebody screamed,"Gun!" Whoever it was had probably seen the man had his hand in his pocket and thought he was going to pull out a weapon. When the guard reached the man, he hit the guard in the nose and started punching him. I knew I had to help. I was not sure if he might really have a gun, but by then I had reached him and shoved him away from the guard. I was ready to fight, but the man fell down, got up, and ran out of the door, followed by other guards.

I turned around to see if my family was all right, and to my surprise, the store, which had been full of people before, was now almost empty, since most of them were hiding behind the counters.

The guard came back and wanted to know if I was all right. I told him I was. He thanked me and told my wife and kids, "Don't ever leave your pocketbook open! Make sure you keep your eyes open all of the time!" and left.

Would you believe? We continued shopping! What we bought, I don't remember—ask my wife when you see her. I'm sure she remembers; if not, my daughter will.

To my daughter, this is what you get for asking. Now you do a good deed that you can remember.

A QUESTION

E VERY TIME I GO to my barber for a haircut, he wants to know what style I want. So I have to tell him how.

I noticed an article the paper once with the headline "Barbecue." I never did read what it means. But as I think about it now, isn't that what I give my barber when he asks what haircut I want, and I tell him that? Isn't that a barber-cue?

REALLY, AM I DEAD?

O NE DAY, WHEN I was younger, a lot younger, I went
to a friend's birthday party. As you know, when
young men get together to party, a very good time is had
by all—at least that's what everybody says, right—eating,
drinking, and bragging about girls and other stuff. I'm
sure I don't have to explain any further.

After celebrating for a few hours, I had enough under
my belt to wonder where the second moon in the sky had
suddenly come from. Unable to figure it out, I said to myself, "I'll leave this puzzle for tomorrow. Today, I'll have
a hard time getting home anyway."

There was an earthquake, too. The street kept twist-
ing back and forth. The funny part was, nobody else noticed it. People keep looking at me. I guessed they were
all drunk, because they did not feel the earthquake. When
I try to warn them, they just laughed.

When I got home, I fell into bed and went to sleep.

Suddenly, I woke up with a jerk. I tried to sit up and
whaaammm! I hit my head. The room was, mysteriously,
very dark, as in a cave. So I reached out to see what I'd
hit with my head. I did not have to reach out too far; a

few inches above me was a wooden ceiling. Then I could feel my left shoulder touching something. It was wooden, too. When I touched the floor and felt that wood, I knew I was in a coffin.

If you think you've ever been scared by something in your life, believe me, I was at that moment ten times more scared. Had I gone into a coma from the drinking, and had they thought I was dead and buried me alive? Had I just awakened, or was this only my soul than had woken up?

Then I heard an indescribably terrible sound. If I was dead, I knew now for sure that I was not going to heaven because angels sing nice songs, with melodies. This sound was, for sure, no singing; it could only be some ghoulish creature from hell coming for me.

Then the light went on, and my mother barked, "What is the matter? Where are you? Why are you screaming?"

That's when I discovered that I was under the bed, and that the terrible sound was coming from my mouth. Ashamed, I came crawling out and said, "Oh, I was only chasing a mouse—it ran under the bed, and I tried to catch it."

My mother took a look at me and said, "The way you were hollering, I'm sure what you chased was some white elephants. Good night!"

How had I gotten under the bed? Who knew; I'd just make sure, before I went to a birthday party from then on, that I put some chairs in front of my bed.

REMINISCENCE

THE OTHER DAY, I was reminiscing with somebody about the Good Old Days. Among other things, we talked how, many years ago when I was still small, a deceased person was laid out in the house and not in the morgue. Deceased? Morgue? Good Old Days? How does that fit together? You were not there, so skip it. It only reminded me about "mourning in the house."

A black curtain was draped around the entrance to the house, similar to the way it is done around a firehouse or police station when a firefighter or police officer dies here. There was always some old woman sitting in the room where the dead person was laid out, telling some morbid stories of how hard some people pass away from accidents, killings, and of ghosts.

Ghosts were invariably one of the main topics. When the hearse arrived and the casket had been carried out of the house, all the chairs were turned upside down, so no soul—or ghost— cold find a place to sit. The chairs remained that way until after the burial.

Now to my real-life story (the way it was conveyed to me by my grandmother). One day a well-known man had died, so the room was quite filled with women and men telling the usual stories. Since the person was more than twenty-four hours dead, his beard had grown some. Oh, yes—a beard keeps growing after death; ask a doctor. His wife wanted him to look good because he had always been so vain while alive, so she called in the barber.

When he came, he had a good ghost story himself. He told it while he was soaping up the dead man's face to soften the hair—not to avoid hurting the dead person, but to keep his razor knife sharp. As the story progressed, the tension grew and the barber's voice got softer and softer. There was not a peep from the audience; the barber, now so involved with the story, got some soap in the dead man's nose without realizing it.

As it turned out, the man was not dead, only in a deep coma. The tickling of the soap in his nose brought him out of the coma, and a really loud sneeze was the result.

Without a sound, the barber jumped out the window. He even took the soap bowl and the brush with him! The women—well, the first and second were silent, and then, as if on command, all got to their feet at the same time. Chairs fell over, and screams shot through the room as their anxiety to escape increased. Too bad; next to the door, a heavy woman was sitting, and she and another women got wedged in the door, blocking the exit.

After some fainting and some bruises, everybody calmed down. Finally, a doctor pronounced the dead person alive, and there was a party.

Only the barber did not attend. Nobody could find him; all they discovered were his soap bowl and brush.

ROCKY

ROCKY IS SIXTY POUNDS of the friendliest dog there is. What kind of dog? How should I know? A rusty-colored dog. My son and his wife got him from a kennel a few years back, and he really is a part of their family. My daughter-in-law has spent many pleasant hours with the dog, teaching him all kinds of tricks—sitting, rolling over, begging, broken legs, etc.

My son frequently has to go on business trips all over the USA, and at times to Puerto Rico and Europe, too. On some of these trips, he takes his wife, and now my grand-son, with him. After concluding his business, he takes a couple of days of vacation for sightseeing.

At such times, we baby-sit the dog.

When Rocky is at our house, he has his "lamb fur" in a little-used room on the floor where he sleeps. In our bedroom, my wife sleeps on the side facing the door. Occasionally, the dog sneaks in and lies down, on that side, on the floor. In the morning we tell him,"No, no—you cannot do this!" He seems to understand, feels guilty, and for the next night sleeps in his room.

Today, at four in the morning, I had to go to the bathroom. As I stepped out of the bed, instead of hitting the floor, I hit something very furry. "Oh, what the heck is this?" I screamed.

Being so rudely awakened by having his tail stepped on, Rocky uttered a shocked "Yip!"

I, in the meanwhile, had fallen back on the bed, my head landing on my wife's stomach. "The ceiling is falling!" she screamed.

Rocky, who had sneaked in during the night, knew it was a no-no to sleep on my wife's side but must have figured it was OK to sleep on mine. She, awakened by a "falling ceiling," jumped out of the bed, and, as Rocky was zipping around the bed and reached her side at that very moment, she landed on him. "Oh! What the heck is that!" she shrieked.

He yipped and yapped again before flying out the door. My wife, having lost her balance, came crashing back on the bed. I was still lying where my head had hit her stomach; down came her behind, with all her might, on me.

Then I was sure that the ceiling was falling.

Even though my ears were muffled with my entire wife on me, I could hear her scream again.

Well, I cannot blame her, it must have goosed her pretty good, and somehow up in the air she went. This act of hers put very painful friction on my earlobes, so I screamed, too.

From somewhere in the house at that moment came a

loud thud—Rocky was moving too fast, could not stop, and hit a wall.

"Ohh! What the heck was that?" Rocky was screaming now. I swear I heard him say it!

We laughed so hard that the bed was shaking. Afterward, I told my wife, "You almost took my ears with you."

She said, "Shave next time. I thought I was sitting on a wire brush."

Now, I'm wondering when she ever sat on a wire brush, to be able to compare my beard with it? But this is probably another story. Finally she asked me "Why did you want to get up?"

I told her, "I don't know, I forgot."

The family, 1917. Clockwise from bottom left: Emilie
Breinich Bader; Anton Breinich, Sr.; Maritzi Breinich, Kathrina
Breinich, Anton Breinich, Matilda Breinich, Emma Breinich,
and Anton Breinich.

The family, 1938. From left, front: Siegfried, Emilie, Margaret, Emma Breinich, Alfred, and Hedwig. Back: Michael
Bader and Anton Breinich.

Werschetz Catholic Church, Yugoslavia, in the 1930s

Our dance group. My wife (third from left) and I (holding the flag) did not know each other then, in 1950, in Salzberg.

Marching as part of the dance group, 1952 (by then, Anna and I knew each other).

Me and my sister Margaret, 1941

Our wedding, April 10, 1955

Our last photo in Austria, with Hannelore, 1956

Christmas at the Simons', 1966

Our Twenty-fifth Wedding Anniversary, 1980

With Henry Baker, 2000

Ramapo Reservation, Mahwah, New Jersey

SCHOOL'S STARTING

HERE'S HOW IT WAS more than seventy years ago, when I was a kid still going to school.

My school was about eight blocks from my home. There were no cars, and there were no buses. You walked. On cold or hot days. Period. We just did, no matter what, since that was the only way you got to school. And a snow day was. . .what? Snow or not, you put on your boots and went. The school was heated, some rooms better than others, depending how far your room was from the furnace—which was built into the wall. There was no air-conditioning either in the good old days.

I can also tell you that you went to school willingly. Your mother took you by your hand, if you were small, or you could go alone if you wanted to. If you did not want to go to school at all, she dragged you there by your arm or by your ear, and then the teacher dragged you in. Nothing could save you, so you just went, no matter what the weather was.

By the time you were in the third grade, you had some fun throwing snowballs at the girls or chasing them home, though, those being the good old days, she might clobber you with her school bag if you did. This, however, heated up your ears in an instant. You think it must have hurt? Probably, though it sure is funny to remember it now.

Today, most kids who go to school live more than two blocks away from it and are transported to it in a bus, or have their mother drive them in an air-conditioned car, or in a heated one when it gets cold, because what self-respecting person would drive two or three blocks in a cold car before it's warmed up?

At the end of the school day, God forbid kids have to walk home in hot or cold weather. There's the bus again, or the mother with the air-conditioning or warm car, even if she has to take off from work to do it. And if there's any real snow, kids get a day off or an early dismissal.

I should have had it so good!

SHOPPING

SOMETIMES I GO FOOD shopping when my wife is for some reason not able (or doesn't want) to go. I prefer to go to the A&P, because the store has self-checkout scanners. There I do not have to talk to anyone—just pay by cash or by credit card at the machine, pack the stuff myself, and be gone without a word a cashier (I'm not one for chitchat in a store).

The other day, my wife wanted some yogurt and didn't want to go to the supermarket. As I was parking in their lot, I saw an old man standing next to his car and giving me an OK sign.

Now what does he want? I wondered. When I got out of the car, I asked, "Is everything all right?"

This was my first mistake. The guy came over and started to talk. "All these young people don't look out for old guys like us. They drive and park so fast, they almost run you over." On and on he went.

I hadn't come there to talk but to shop, so I just said, "Yeah, you're right," and started walking.

Don't underestimate an old man who wants to talk. He followed me and kept grumbling and grumbling about these young people nowadays.

Luckily for me, another old man was leaving the store, pushing his shopping cart. He turned his attention to this guy. I guess my "Yeah, you're right" hadn't satisfied a need. Before I entered the store, I looked back, and there they were in deep discussion, right in the driveway, not noticing that some cars were trying to pass. One car with a young guy in it tooted his horn for them to move.

"Oh, this young generation—no time at all!"

"Humph! That proves it!"

While I was shopping for all kinds of food, I looked for the yogurt for my wife, the cheap one. I ignored the seventy-five-cent brand one, selected two for fifty cents each, and proceeded to the self-checkout scanners. All of my purchases went through the scanner without a hitch, but one of the two yogurts did not. I asked the young woman who was on duty there for some help. She put a key in the machine, and it turned out the yogurt was not in the program. I asked her, "How come one went through and the other didn't?"

She looked. One was peach-flavored and the other strawberry. I told her to forget about it, but she sent somebody to check. In the meantime, I had some other people behind me impatiently waiting for the machine, so I paid for the rest but only for one yogurt.

After I had paid and packed my stuff and was ready to go home, the women came back and said that this yogurt was fifty-nine cents, and I should have had two of the same—either for fifty or fifty-nine cents each, that that had been my mistake, "But just come over here to the cash register—you can get it here."

I was in no mood for more talk, and went over and gave her a dollar just to get it over with. I paid the fifty-nine cents.

"How are you?" she asked

More talk; to say something, I said, "OK, but it could be better."

That was mistake number two. She wanted to know, "How could it be better?"

What had I let myself in for? What should I tell her?

The old-guy and young-guy dilemma came to mind, so I said, "If I were just thirty years younger, it would be much better. But then I'd have to go to work again!"

She opened her mouth really wide—I could see her tonsils—and a burst of laughter (like a horse neighing) came out so ear-splittingly loud that I almost got scared. All the people started to look at us; I took my second yogurt, and the forty-one cents, and hurried out.

As I passed another loading her cart at the checkout, she looked at me as if she was going to ask what I had said to the clerk because she could use a laugh, too. Oh, please—not another talk! I was thinking.

I marched past her like a train in full steam. Would you believe that those three guys were still there talking? I wonder, was it now about their wives?

Next time my wife wants a yogurt, she'll have to get it herself.

SIE SCHREIT SCHON WIEDER!

A S THEY SAY, "WHEN you get older, you start to remember your younger years." I'm into remembering now, but this doesn't make me older, does it?

When I was about five years old and my sister, a little baby at that time, was a couple of months old, for some reason I will never know she got into these crying spells. Nothing calmed her down; my mother had to take her out of the house in her carriage and push her around in front, which was the only thing that helped.

Every time she started to cry, we said in German, "*Sie schreit schon wieder*")("She's screaming again"). In one of these crying spells, when they came out into the yard, I was playing there with my new Lederhosen and my pistols. A Lederhosen is a short pair of pants made of deer leather and held up with suspenders crossed in the front with an embroidered bib (Austrian style). I was shooting some imaginary robbers or Indians.

I had two regular cap pistols of the type you still can buy, a little version of the Western kind that bad guys would hide with to kill the good guy when they took his pistol away. Or ladies would carry a real one just my size, in their "secret places," for protection. I holstered mine like a cowboy.

The Lederhosen and the Western guns did not exactly fit together as an outfit, but I did not care. For me, they were perfect. When I went out in this outfit to play, I was reminded by my parents, "Keep your Lederhosen clean." Nobody cared about whether my guns would get dirty or break.

I liked the small pistol—it made a loud bang, almost like a real gun. The noise came from a paper-type round plug, filled with sulfur, which was pushed into the front of the barrel of the pistol like a cork into a bottle. When the trigger was pulled, a spring drove a nail in the gun into the sulfur, which exploded and spit fire.

That late afternoon, I was having my fun as an Austrian cowboy when my mother and sister emerged because *"Sie schreit schon wieder."* Seeing me, Mother told me to put my guns away. "No noise, so your sister can fall asleep."

I had just put a new plug into the barrel and wondered what to do with the gun. I put it in my Lederhosen pocket.

From time to time I put my hand into the pocket to check if the pistol was still there. As I stood there next to the carriage, looking at my sister finally and blissfully sleeping, I checked again and somehow pulled the trigger. *Kaboom* it went, and luckily the gun must have been pointed to the pants side and not to my leg.

The pants suddenly had a big hole and were burning.

I started screaming, and my mother was screaming even louder, though my sister kept sleeping.

My mother ripped the burning pants off me and discovered I had only a little burn on my leg. But the pants, the ones I had to be so careful with, were dirty, burned, and ruined. I did not put them on again—at least I don't remember doing so. Come to think of it, I cannot remember if my sister had these "*Sie schreit schon wieder*" spells after that. Maybe the gun episode cured her.

SOMETHING FOUL IN THE STORE

THE OTHER DAY I went to a well-known department store—not for something in particular; I don't know what I need until I see it. Then, aha!—enlightenment comes. How did I survive without it for so long? Now I know this is what I came for, and, so I won't run out of it, I buy two.

So far that day I had not encountered my I Have To Have This Today moment. So I wandered around in the aisles, hanging half over the shopping cart.

As I turned into one aisle, there was an elderly woman standing at the other end. I had not gone two feet when she started to run away at full speed.

What had I done to scare her so much? As I reached the end of the aisle, I suddenly realized. It was not me scaring her but something much more overpoweringly urgent to her, because the aroma in the air was so strong. In four words, it stank like hell. I could see her disappear into the restroom with her hand suspiciously behind her back.

So there I was, standing in that smell. I swung my cart around to go as fast as possible. Another woman came around the corner just then and got a good whiff of this smell too, but, not having seen the real culprit disappear, she looked at me as if I was to blame.

What to do now? Should I tell her, "Hey, it wasn't me—I'm innocent!" Would she believe it?

I took the easy way out and followed the example of the first woman—ran away, too.

Later this woman met me in another aisle. The air was much better there, but her glances at me were the same. Needless to say, it was the end of my shopping, because if I had met her again, she might pass me with her hand to her nose.

When you go in a store, you go to get something, right? But I'm sure, innocent as you are, it's not dirty looks you're shopping for.

SOMETHING TO THINK ABOUT
(WHILE YOU SIT THERE)

FROM CHILDHOOD ON, YOUR mother and father (father not so much) remind you to wash your hands after you go the bathroom.

Subsequently in life, many people tell you the same: the teacher, the doctor, and everybody else. In some toilets, there is the reminder powerfully displayed on the walls to wash your hands before you leave. And of course, you, as an orderly person, do always wash your hands before you leave a toilet.

Now, when you get up off the toilet, your underpants have to be pulled up, right? Then the pants go up, and the undershirt has to be tucked into it. All the rest of the clothes have to be adjusted, too. Don't you think your hands are by then wiped clean, with all this tugging and pulling on your clothes? How come we still do have to wash the hands?

Come to think of it, just keep washing your hands as I do, need to or not. It will make your mother happy, and, if nothing else, that will make you feel better!

And while we're on the subject, how come we don't have to put on clean clothes after we've washed our hands?

Or are you doing that?

THE NEWSPAPER,
MY MORNING ROUTINE

Every day, after I get up in the morning, I go for the *Record* of Bergen County. The newspaper is delivered by car in the night, and the driver throws it out the window in to the driveway as he is passes each house. The paper is in a plastic bag that slides smoothly on the asphalt, so it isn't damaged.

This time, it had rained, and the paper was soaking wet. Usually, the paper gets double-bagged then and stays dry. It must have started to rain after the delivery, and the paper was only in a single bag.

Now what? I hate to break my routine. I want to read the paper with my coffee at breakfast. So my wife said she would hang it outside to dry on the wash line. But that would take too long, I thought, and to call the *Record* for a new copy would take just as long. I decided to go for a new paper in the supermarket. It costs only a buck and a half, I told myself, and I can get my breakfast faster.

Once in the store, I saw some grapes; well, I'm here, I figured, so I put a package in the cart. Then, "Hah, the fish I like!" It was on sale too, and I get a pound and a half. . . . And guess what? The seltzer's on sale, too . . . in the cart with it. You think only one bottle? No, I'll take six. Oh, rice pudding! Haven't had any for a long time. It'll be great for breakfast!

To make the story short, I found more things, and only as I was putting it all on the belt at the checkout counter did I remember the newspaper!

So I put the items in the cart back on the belt, got the paper, and returned check-out.

My dollar-fifty paper had bloomed to over twenty-nine dollars, but the paper was dry, and I had all those other goodies, and it'd taken me only a hour and a half in the store. Home to breakfast!

My wife had the coffee ready; I put some rice pudding in a dish and opened the paper on the table, but before I could eat and read it, I had to get a glass of water for my medication. I was awfully hungry by then—and I clipped the rice pudding dish with the water glass, and the glass slipped out of my hand—and poured all over the paper!

I wondered what to do next. Get another paper? What guarantee, I asked myself, do I have that it will not get wet a third time? Or should I go out to eat and then read a newspaper at the restaurant?

Then I remembered my wife had hung the first paper outside on her wash line.

Some of the pages were dry, so I figured I might as well read them at least. I grabbed what I could. This worked out perfectly until one story was continued on page 9, and another to page 11, both of which were still wet.

You get the idea. By the time everything was dry and I was finished with the paper that day, it was going on supper time.

I think I should have called the newspaper for a replacement. It would have been faster and cheaper.

THE BIGGEST SURPRISE IN MY LIFE

MY BIGGEST SURPRISE WAS when—well, I did see it coming. My biggest surprise is, at the moment, that I cannot recall any surprises at all.

When you get as old as I am, a big surprise is that I'm still here—maybe not the biggest of unexpected occurrences but a happy one for me, so I just keep on breathing and, hopefully, make my wife and daughters and son, and all my grandchildren, happy, too, maybe?

So when you read what I have written, I hope you will have a happy moment too and not fall asleep.

Wait a minute! Now I remember a surprise. When I came to the U.S.A., my English was practically nonexistent, so I had a hard time finding a doctor and a dentist.

Just think: You see a doctor and have some complaint, you have, let's say, a case of diarrhea, but you don't speak English. You don't know how to tell him what's the matter. Maybe just pointing to your rear-end and saying. "Pit, pit, plash, and spit," won't do. Or you maybe have something on your body that hurts; do you just undress and point? "Here's where it hurts," you intend to say. "Can you see this, Doctor?" This is before he even knows you or what you have, all this without him telling you, "Take your clothes off!"

Thankfully, I was given the address of a physician who spoke German.

But the dentist—there wasn't a German-speaking one around, and one of the molars way in the back of my mouth hurt me badly. The dentist I found was a real old man (at least as I saw "old" at the young age I was then).

When I entered his office, to my great surprise he had some teeth missing himself, and he had a really tall bird stand in the office close to his desk which had a big perching ring on the top of its stand with a big parrot sitting on it.

But the pain made me stay there. When I was sitting in the chair, I just opened my mouth, moved my finger to the tooth, and said, "Ouch!" At this point the parrot started to yammer as if he was getting a tooth pulled. (You can teach a parrot to say anything as long it hears it repeated often enough.)

The dentist took a look, left me, then came back with an enormous needle, and said something I did not understand, so he opened his mouth wide to show me what to do. I did, and then the needle went in once, then again, and there was the surprise: It went through my gum and came out through my cheek. I could feel the outside of my cheek getting wet from what was in the needle.

"Oops!" the dentist said.

I would have said it too, but try to say "oops" with a needle in your mouth. I didn't need to say anything, though—the parrot started to yammer again as if he'd been shot.

And the tooth got pulled, and—surprise, surprise—I did not get any infection. I heard that that dentist had retired soon after. Well, as I said, he was old.

THE BUTTERFLY

S HE SHEDS HER COCOON, and her body gains strength. She is no longer, in the first stage of her life, like a small child, a caterpillar; she has grown up into a beautiful butterfly. Her wings flex and they are full of colors. Her legs let go of the plant where the metamorphosis occurred, and she is off in the air, flying.

Worlds of impressions are opening for her. The different colors of the flowers, the breeze in the air, the warmth of the sun, and she is navigating to fly here or there, and above all the scent of food is everywhere. Instinctively, she flies to the right flowers and tastes the sweet nectar of it for the first time in her life.

While she is feeding on the flower, a kitten notices her. Oh, it thinks, there is something to play with! It stalks and crawls closer and closer, then jumps.

Luckily the butterfly had good eyes, and at the last moment she soars up in the air and gets away. There are several more close calls with birds and children, but she's fast and gets away each time.

Later in the day, she finds other butterflies of her kind. They are soon flying, playing, and dancing together, having a good time.

Then the time comes to lay her eggs; carefully she chooses a spot for them. After that, there's more eating and playing, till night comes.

It's cold then, with no sun to warm her. Although she has a dry spot under an overhang of a house, she's freezing. So she dreams of tomorrow, when the sun will shine. She will fly higher, eat and play more than ever before, and all will be much better.

In the morning the sun comes out, and soon enough she's warming up, just as she dreamed. So she casts off to fly higher and better. Somehow, though, it's not as easy—it's harder to fly.

Maybe she has to eat to gain some strength, but the food does not taste as good either. Getting away from the birds is also very clumsy, more luck than wisdom. She sees other butterflies playing, but she has no interest.

Suddenly her wings do not carry her any more, and she falls to the ground. She struggles to get up again, realizing in the end it is useless. She remembers yesterday, when her wings carried her where she wanted to go, playing with her friends, all the fullness of life, and the fun. As life slowly fades out of her, she realizes that, for her, there is only a yesterday; tomorrow never will be, was only a dream.

So live for today, for when today turns into a yesterday, it could be too late, and maybe tomorrow will never come.

THE CAR KEYS

ID YOU EVER LOCK your car keys in the car? Even with the engine running? No, of course not. You are one of the exceptions. You're one of the level-headed ones. You think ahead: Pull the key out of the ignition before closing the door. And, although it could happen once in a blue moon to you too, I'm sure you have a spare key with you to open the door.

I'm not that smart, I confess. I've locked myself out a couple of times. Having no spare key with me, what is there to do? The moment that I heard the thud of a door closing, with the lock buttons pushed down. . .well? Looking through the window at the ignition key still stuck in the place, I stood there, scratching the head and praying to all the saints I could remember for help. That's about it.

One day my wife and I went to visit our in-laws in Queens. After parking the car, I pulled the key out of the ignition and put it in my pocket. As I was leaving the car, I pushed the door lock button down. Then my wife complained that I'd parked too close to the tree, that it was too hard for her to get out of the car. So I got back in the car, started it, pulled back two feet, got out of the car and thud, thud—both doors closed. This time I'd forgotten to pull the key out of the ignition.

The police, Triple A, and a mechanic could not open the doors unless they broke a window, because my car had theft-preventive cups installed. The consequence was that my son-in-law had to drive to my house in Mahwah, New Jersey, to get a spare key—a round trip that took three and a half hours!

After another of this type of head-scratching situation and calling my wife up to bring me a key, I got smart. I put an ignition key in my wallet. Then I had an idea. The next time I went shopping with my wife, I was going to play a prank on her: lock the key in the car, and go through the head-scratching and all the yammering that goes with that. Then when my wife was really angry at me, ta-da! I'd pull the key out of my wallet.

Dumb idea, you say?

On the way to the store, I stopped for gas in a good mood for my upcoming joke. After I paid for the gas, I even tipped the station attendant a quarter.

At the store, I intentionally left the key in the ignition, we got out of the car, I pushed the lock button and thud, thud, the doors were closed.

"Oh, boy, oh, boy—I left the key in the ignition again!" I exclaimed, starting to scratch my head.

My wife asked, "You what? Tell me again."

"OK, I left my key –"

"Oh, be quiet! Let me see if this is the truth."

She walked around the car and took a look at the ignition lock!

I would like to tell all the glorious names she had for me at that time, but this is another story.

"See, my dear," I at last told her, "all this excitement is not necessary, and why? Because you have a very smart husband—me."

She looked doubtfully at me.

In triumph, I went into my pocket for my wallet and . . .I couldn't find it.

I didn't understand—I paid for the gas, I told myself, and laid my wallet on the seat because. . . . Oh, boy, oh, boy! It was hard to put it back into my pocket because the seatbelt was around me, so I'd laid it next to me on the seat. And my spare key is in the wallet, and the wallet is on the seat—in the locked car!!

The prayer to all my dear saints did not help much.

After explaining the situation to my wife, would you know, she was laughing. This was all wrong—I should be laughing now. How come it was so humiliating?

She went shopping, and I went on a three-mile walk home to get a spare key. At least when I got home, I figured, I could use my wife's car to drive back.

When I got home, I found the spare key for my car but not the keys to my wife's car. As it turned out, I had to walk the three miles back, too. She had both of the keys to her car in her pocketbook. How come none of mine?

I did not ask her, because after the six-mile walk, I did not have the energy.

Trust me, since then wherever I go, I carry two wallets in my pants pockets, with a spare key in each. Nobody is going to laugh at me because I locked myself out of a car again. The only problem is, my pants have gotten heavier from the two wallets, so I've had to tighten my belt some more. That makes me looked skinnier, but with heavy bulging pants pockets, something to really laugh about. (I cannot win!)

THE CHASE

M ANY TIMES WHEN MY granddaughter, Cerrie, who was in sixth grade, came home from school, I heard her complaining about what the boys had done that day. Christina, her mother, tried to console her by saying, "They do that because they like you,"or, "Ignore it," depending on the complaint—whether it was a tease or a torment from the boys.

"Punch him in the nose," I told her.

You're probably thinking, How can he give such violent advice to a girl?

I'm reminded of a time when I was about eight or nine years old. Many, many years have passed since then, and I can't even remember the names of all the kids involved, but let me tell you the story anyway.

We were three boys, chasing three girls after school (there were no school buses at that time). It was always the same; the girls left together, and so did the boys. When we came out of the building, the chase began. Although I lived closest to the school, I had to chase Susie, who lived the farthest away. Why? God only knows; I sure didn't.

We all had our books in some type of attaché case,

which was pressed tight under our arms, and off we went. If we came too close and there was a chance that we might catch the girls, they started to scream too loud. So we would fall back, but not so much that the girls were not scared either, or the hollering or the fun would stop altogether.

As each girl reached her house, the boy who had chased her left for his home. Since I lived only one block from the school and the girl that I chased lived about a mile from it, I had plenty of time on my way home to wonder, Why am I doing this? So every day I resolved after the chase, "No more." However, it did not last. The next day it was the same thing. That is, until she'd had enough of the game.

This day, the other four kids were already home. Only Susie and I had to finish. Susie had just run around the corner to enter her street, which caused me to lose sight of her temporarily. I was only a few feet behind. So, all I had to do was get around the corner, run about another five houses, then she was home and my job would be done.

But as I rounded the corner, *wham!* Something hit me on the head. The next moment I was sitting on the ground. What the heck had happened? Had a tree moved onto the sidewalk, and had I run into it?

As I glanced up, I could see Susie taking another swing with her attaché case. Hey, that was supposed to be under her arm, and she was supposed to be running! Lightning fast, I understood. The chase had ended. Before the attaché case could reach me for a second time, I was up and running in the other direction. All I could feel was a mighty wind passing my head as the attaché case whistled past.

That day I'm sure I would have qualified for the Olympics—running home faster than ever before, scared to look back because Susie could be behind me swinging her attaché case.

I never chased Susie again. The next day she was as sweet as honey, and we were even good friends after that. I, for my part, had had my first lesson of the opposite sex: one day a whammy, the next, "Hi, sugar, how are you?" You think you understand women, but you really don't!

The other two chased "their girls" for two more days. I informed them, "I'm tired of it." On the third day, one of the other boys came to school, mumbling something: "No more chasing because of a headache." Needless to say, we both knew where his headache had come from—and our unwillingness to continue the chase.

So sexual harassment can start very young. But a punch from a girl at the right time can teach a young Casanova, "Back off"! a lesson I never forgot that will stay with me for the rest of my life. Believe me, when my wife says "Whoa, stop!" now I say, "Yes, dear."

THE CONVERTIBLE

E VERY PERSON IN THE world, I'm sure, has a dream to own something someday that is, for whatever reason, at the moment out of reach. Some are lucky and get all their dreams fulfilled. Others, the unlucky ones, get none, though most of us, the in-between, get some.

One of my dream items was to own a convertible. I did not have my dream fulfilled until the mid-Sixties. Never mind that the car was a few years old and needed some engine repair, and that the canvas roof was not in too good a shape. Never mind that I was married and had four children to put in a back seat with room for only two persons.

The convertible was a red Ford at a price I could afford. The engine repair I could do myself, so I bought it. Every time there was an opportunity, my wife and I put the children in the back seat, practically in each other's lap, and off we drove.

My children are now all grown up but probably still wonder: Why did he have a convertible when he never put the roof down? Let me answer this question with another one: "Which two of the four would have wanted to stay home? When we went for a drive to go somewhere, the roof, when it was down, took up more space in the rear seat, and there really would not have been room for four kids. So the roof came down only on the rarest occasions, that is, if I could sneak a ride with my wife alone. This was good anyway, because the material of that roof, as I said before, was in poor shape.

How poor I discovered that first winter. It snowed overnight, and the snow pushed the roof really deep into the car. We wanted to go shopping, so I carefully removed the snow as much as possible, stuffed the kids in the back seat, and off we went.

Since I did not dare to remove the snow all the way to the canvas, the weight pushed the roof so low that it was sitting on my head. Hoping that the wind would blow off the snow as I drove, I drove on. After three miles, I realized this was only wishful thinking, on top which it started to snow again. So I asked my wife to push the snow off by tapping the canvas from the inside lightly while I was driving.

Well, my wife's light tapping was. . .if you ever saw somebody executing a karate chop, then you know what I mean. Needless to say, her hand went right through the roof, snow and all, so her arm was protruding like the periscope on a submarine.

For a few seconds both of us were speechless; then she calmly pulled her hand in again, turned to me, and said: "See what you made me do?"

I could not answer, because the wind got hold of the

hole in the roof and, with a crack, part of the roof was ripping away. As a result, all the snow from the roof landed in our laps. I think I heard some wisecracks from my children in the back: "Never seen such a terrific snowball fight."

"Fight? You mean an avalanche."

After pulling to the side and cleaning all the snow out of the car, I checked the roof. There was nothing I could do. Half of the canvas was folded back, resting on the still-intact other half. At least the children were still covered.

I had to do drive another mile to a U-turn, get to the other side of the road, and go home. When we picked up a little speed, the wind finished off the rest of the roof— the canvas, totally off the top, bolted only to the body of the car, was flying like a large flag behind us, waving in the wind.

Now picture this: in the middle of the winter, while snowing, somebody is driving in a convertible with four children and a woman. The roof is down, dragging behind the car like a black flag waving in the wind to make sure that everybody sees them. Other cars lowered their windows and called out all kinds of remarks. We, of course, could not show defeat, so we shouted back, "Happy Easter" and "Have a good Fourth of July."

In hindsight, my children cannot say I never took them out in our convertible without the top down.

THE DRAIN PROBLEM

FOR SEVERAL DAYS WHEN I took my shower, I noticed that the water was draining slowly from the bathtub. There must be too much of my wife's long hair and soap scum in the drain, I concluded. So I went to the supermarket for drain cleaner.

There were several brands for sale, and I was looking for something good, so I studied all the products. Every brand advertised how good it was, but one also said it was "professional strength," and that the entire plumbing union was using it. How wrong could you go if all the plumbers were using the stuff? I bought a gallon of it.

That night, before I went to sleep, I poured half the can into the drain, and the other half early in the morning. Then I waited an hour before I took my shower. That's when I discovered I should never, ever again buy that stuff.

I turned the shower on, and as soon I got in and was standing there—but remained as dry as I had been when I entered, because that drain cleaner had opened the drain so well, it was sucking the water straight off the shower head and down the drain without making me wet.

What to do? I told my wife to sit down, cut some hair from her head with a pair of scissors, mixed the hair with some soap, and stuffed it all into the drain to slow it down.

I might have cut off too much of my wife's hair, because she complained that she now looked like a plucked chicken. I told her this was necessary for the good of the family.

When I turned on the water in the shower again, the drain did not drain at all, and I realized that I had indeed removed too much of her hair, and had plugged up the drain again.

I went to the supermarket and bought a milder drain cleaner. Now when I get my shower, the water drains off OK.

All would have been just about all right, but my wife complained about a sunburn she'd gotten on her head because I'd cut off too much hair. I went yet again to the supermarket again, this time to buy some hair-growing product.

Then a horrible thought came to me: What if I get some of this hair-growing product on her face? Will she have to shave from then on? So I went to a kiddy store and bought a mask to cover her face while I did the hair—you know, the president look-alike sort (she looked like Nixon).

In three months, she will have her hair back again, too. All's well when it ends well. Which it did.

THE EARLY SHOW

I WAS ONCE WATCHING THE *Early Show* in bed in the morning. Sometimes I have a hard time falling asleep at night—we have a TV in the bedroom—and then I turn it on with a twenty-minute timer, my guarantee for going to sleep before the twenty minutes are up and the TV goes off, because all the shows on TV nowadays sure put me to sleep.

If I don't do this and leave the TV off, I may stay awake for thirty minutes or more, even an hour, and, when I do try to go to sleep, toss and turnover and over again.

While I was watching the Early Show, my wife was up already and had come back from whatever she was doing and lay down on her side of the bed to watch with me. There was the usual programming news, stuff that had happened the day before, the weather report, and so on, and my wife was very quickly asleep and snoring.

It would not have taken much, and I would have been asleep again too, even in the morning—the TV was not that good. Then I heard something about some women, coming on next, not too happy with their sex lives.

I was instantly wide awake again. It was some kind

of a course they took to enhance their sex lives. The teacher said that all the men whose female partners were taking this course had to go to play golf when the class was scheduled.

I had no idea what women have to go through to have a satisfactory sex life. They had to exercise their legs one at a time and bend them back at the knee so the heel of the foot made contact with their behinds, like a runner does to loosen up before a run. Then they had to do stuff I had never seen, even in an aerobics class. I just could mentally see the husband standing by and twirling his thumbs, until one of them was finished with all that exercise, to get into the mood (I wondered if he didn't change his mood by then).

Then the teacher faced one of the women (the best-looking one, naturally) and locked the fingers of both his hands with the woman's. He took some dance steps back and forth for a while, raising his right arm high over his head, then his left arm too, then lifting both her arms with his locked fingers so high she had to stand on her toes.

I'd had enough, gotten the idea, and I rose, moved to my wife's side of the bed, and asked her to get up, "Why, what do you want?" she asked.

"You'll see," I said.

I locked my fingers with hers, raised her right arm, then the left, then both arms. Then I looked deep into her eyes and asked, "Are you ready now?"

She grabbed a pillow and started to beat me with it.

(I guess she understood what I was doing but wasn't ready.) That pillow landed all over me.

That wasn't what they'd been showing on TV! No wife had been instructed to beat her husband with a pillow, so far as I could tell. Believe me, though, beating me with the pillow was good exercise for my wife; exhausted, she fell back on the bed and went to sleep again.

They should include this pillow beating in their exercise program, I think.

I turned off the TV.

THE ELECTRIC CARS

Y OU CAN'T OPEN A paper, or watch the news on TV, or read a magazine, without hearing about the bright future of the electric cars and how much better they are. Cars will save so much gas and money to drive; so much energy will be saved. Chevrolet has the Volt, Nissan the Leaf, and Ford and BMW, and I don't know how many more, are getting into the act.

This sounds really good until you see the price of the car, and see how many miles you get on a charge.

The way I see it, to get somewhere, you have to charge the car's batteries. But what if you have all the breaker slots off the electric outlets in your house are used up? Or the car maybe needs a stronger burst of electricity than your wiring can take? Hello, electrician. It is said that some battery charges can use as much electricity as the rest of the house. What if you go to faraway places and the battery dies? Oh, there will be charger stations just like gas stations, you say. To gas up is annoying if you're behind some other cars and have to wait for a pump to get free, but you are on your way in a few minutes. Could you do that if your auto battery take hours to charge?

What then? Change the battery? This takes time too, though, and you might get one much older than yours installed; will that make you happy?

What if, across the street and two houses down, they start to plug in to charge their car, and a hundred other people in town do, too? You're watching your favorite show on TV and, poof!it all goes dark. Just a little overload, the electric company will tell you. We didn't have enough capacity generated; it will be better in two days (if there's no snow storm).

What if your neighbor comes and brags about how much he saves on gas and how much less he pollutes? Does he tell why you have to pay more for electricity, the price of which went up because of higher usage by all the electrical cars?

You will pay more, you can be sure, for electricity, and more for all the new electric power plants they'll have to build, so your neighbor can save.

Will there be a saving, in the end, for you and me? I don't think so; only the dealers and car companies, and the electric companies, will save big, not you or your neighbor.

And what about all the pollution the electric companies themselves create, and the generators which have to be added to deliver the electricity when it's needed? They run mostly on coal, which is the dirtiest fuel imaginable. So where is the clean air to come from?

I wrote this in 1978.

THE GERMANIC SIEGFRIED

MY GRANDDAUGHTER WANTS TO know what the name Siegfried means; here's a long story made short about it.

A long time ago, the old Germanic tribes had, like the Romans and the Greeks, their own mythology. The supreme Germanic god was Wotan. The god Donner had a mighty hammer, and, when he was fighting and hurled this hammer, lightning and thunder followed. The Germanic equivalent of the Roman goddess Venus was Freia. In German Thursday is still Donnerstag, the day of Donner, and Friday, Freitag, is Freia's day. (In English, this becomes "Friday," through Anglo-Saxon, the early language of the Germanic tribes that settled in Britain.)

One of the great Germanic myths is the *Nibelungen* saga, in which a large Germanic tribe whose king had a daughter named Kriemhild. She was abducted by a dragon and held as a prisoner. The king promised her to any knight who could free her, but no one could—whoever tried was killed by the dragon.

But a knight named Siegfried was able to kill the dragon. He then undressed and took a bath in the dragon's blood. He did not realize that an oak leaf had fallen and stuck to his back, right between the shoulders, while he was doing so. This small area was not bathed in that blood, which shielded the rest of his body by hardening his skin and protected him, from then on, against any weapon. Spears, sabers, arrows, lancets—nothing could penetrate his skin and hurt him. Only the spot where the leaf had lain remained unprotected and vulnerable.

He married Kriemhild and was wining many battles but (like in all the movies nowadays) there was another girl called Brunhilde who wanted Siegfried. Because she could not have him, she wanted him killed, so she got a bad knight to help her, and this knight discover his vulnerability. The knight then set a trap and killed Siegfried.

About two hundred years ago, Richard Wagner, a German composer, composed an opera about this, because at that time there were no movies; otherwise, who knows? It might have been a movie, too.

Siegfried is one of the key characters in that opera. Can you beat that? Here in America, though, as I mentioned earlier, after my first boss, who couldn't pronounce "Siegfried"and insisted on calling me "Fred," his mother, who was German, refused to speak one word to me in the German language—why, I never knew.

As to the meaning of the name, "*sieg*" in German means "winning," or "conquering," and "*frieden*" means "peace," so "Siegfried" means "conquering peace." How much more peaceful meaning can there be in a name?

THE HIKE

SINCE I'D WALKED EVERY day for a few weeks round the pond in the Bergen County Reservation, I felt I exercised enough for a hike in one of the Ramapo Hills.

On my daily walks I pass a little brook with a bridge over it and a trail leading to a hill in the woods. Today I picked this trail. When I looked at the hill from a distance, I estimated it to be about five to six hundred feet high. I thought, How much of a challenge can it be to get to the top of this hill? After crossing the bridge and hiking a couple hundred feet on fairly flat ground, the trail turned quite steep up the hill. About twenty minutes into the hike, I could see the crest.

"Hey!" I said to myself, "that wasn't hard at all. Boy, I must be in better shape than I thought. Next time I'll tackle a mountain in the Bear Mountain Range." In the twenty minutes to get to the top, I stopped only three times to see the view. But there was no view; every time I stopped I gasped, "V-i-e-w-w-w! I'm out of breath!" But don't tell anybody.

As my head finally rose above the hill crest—wait a minute, I discovered, there's another hill, higher than this one, and the trail leads straight to the top of it. The first hill blocked my sight of the real top. To reach that one, I had to stop five times for the view. Then there was yet another higher hill. This must definitely be the top of the hill, I figured, or will the trail go over it and continue like on the first two tops?

A cold shiver ran down my spine. I could turn around, admit defeat, or go on and maybe get lost. Or be eaten by a bear or something. "What am I?" I finally asked myself, "a man or a mouse?"

I could swear I heard my body say, "Marshmallow," but I went on.

I was once told by a friend, "If you get lost in the woods, look for moss on the trees—the moss always faces north." I'd better look for the moss, I concluded, just in case. My hill had two wests, two easts, or two south, but no north, because I could not find moss on any tree. Maybe I'm at the North Pole, I thought. From there, is everything south. Since there are no trees on the North Pole, however, I had to discard that theory. On my next walk, I'd bring a magnifying glass with me to find the moss.

In about forty-five minutes, I reached a rocky cliff. The scene was worth all the effort I had put in to get there. Until that moment, all I could see was the surrounding trees—now I could see many, many more trees from there. Actually, I could see, not only some of Mahwah and Ramsey, but all the way to New York City. The day was clear so the Empire State Building, the Twin Towers, and many more buildings were visible.

I sat down on a tree trunk lying on the ground to eat my sandwich. From time to time I had a creeping feeling going up my legs. Must be from the strain of the walk, I thought.

But when I started to have the same feeling farther up on my body, I finally looked down and discovered that I was sitting on an anthill. Believe me, I did a pretty good dance without any music for a while.

After another half hour of hiking, I still hadn't reached the top. Then the trail started to go downhill. I didn't mind if I didn't get to the top by then, to tell you the truth, as long I did not have to go uphill anymore. Downhill, fine, thank you—thank you to whoever had made the trail.

In a few minutes it passed through a clearing where the gas company had cleared about a forty-foot through the trees, straight from the top to the bottom of the hill, for its pipe line. And on the bottom, in the distance, I could see a paved road that I know would take me back to my car.

A surge of energy went through me; with long strides, I left the trail for the clearing and made my way down the hill. In about fifteen minutes I'd be down, in another twenty at my car, and then home to have a rest. I could not only feel it already, I could taste it.

On the bottom of the hill the clearing ended, and then the shock came. There were houses with fences and *No*

Trespassing signs all over. And behind the fences there might be dogs, and I— "Oh, help!"— had to climb up the clearing again to get back on the trail.

I got to the trail again with a lot of *viieewing* in an hour. I did not dare to go forward; I just backtracked to the cliff and bridge.

Finally I reached my car. The total walk had been four hours, and I never reached the top of the hill. My legs were like two rubber hoses; I was not sure if I would be able to push the gas pedal.

Somehow I made it home. Bear Mountain can wait. If I should decide to go, I will take a magnifying glass with me to find north, and two knee guards, just in case I have to crawl home.

THE POPULATION EXPLOSION

THE EARTH SUMMIT IN Rio de Janeiro 1992 was about how the population explosion has ended, and some call it a success. Most people don't give a damn and are most likely bored by it all, but please stay with me for a while. You may find something interesting about one of the reasons the Earth is in this mess, to which insufficient attention has been paid.

I was born in 1931. The population of the Earth at that time was about 2 billion—a two with nine zeros.

Twenty-five years later (1956), there were 2.5 billion people in the world. Although we'd had a World War in between, with tens of millions of military and civilian casualties, the population had still increased by 500 million.

Thirty three years later (1989), that population had reached 5 billion.

By 1992, the number stood 5.5 billion; in the intervening sixty-one years since my birth, the world's population had thus nearly doubled. From 1989 to 1992, it increased by the same amount as it took from 1931 to 1956.

If you lived 5,500,000,000 seconds, you'd be 160

years old. The average paperback book, similarly, is about an inch thick, and 5.5 billion inches adds up to close to a book a million miles thick.

An astronaut could have traveled to the moon and back one thousand four hundred times to reach that number of miles.

This also means every village, town, or city that existed on earth in 1931 had to be built all over again by 1992 because we needed double the living space. What must this have done to the fields, forests, and the soil?

Think what doubling of the population brought. I don't even have to add the new chemical discoveries of the post-war period, the oil spills, the destroying of forests to make room for living space, and the disruption of the ecology and environment in general that are added to the spills on earth. Is there a wonder that we are in our present mess?

In World War II, about 60 million people got killed. How horrible and tragic wars can be, I don't have to explain, but let say a switch is flipped and half the population of the Earth disappears—we would still have the population we had forty years ago. Or we would have to have eighty-three world wars to reduce the population to that pre-war level. Don't misunderstand me—I don't advocate war, I only want to show how severe the population growth is.

If trends, which have slowed but not changed, continue, we will in the not-too-distant future be facing a world population of 10 million when we still haven't recovered from dealing with five. Imagine doubling all those towns and cities yet again.

If an organism has an internal growth, and this is not stopped, by getting larger and larger the growth poisons and destroys this organism's internal organs, vessels, and bloodstream. We call that cancer. But are we not acting like a cancer on the Earth? Are we not destroying by polluting the air, water, and ground, or, simply growing unchecked, destroying our planet by sheer weight of numbers? How do we dare call ourselves the peak of creation? Look around: Is this not the way to destroy all of creation? We will have to change if we want to lead creation and not remain its cancer—and change fast, if it is not too late already.

It was pointed out during a recent summit that a child born in the West consumes thirty-seven times the resources of the Earth than a child born in the third world. So this Western child will pollute and deplete global resources that much more. This suggests, of course, that it is justifiable to have so many children in third-world countries.

Yes, this is to a point true; a child here will drive a car, use more oil, electricity, etc. We must also consider, though, that we only have that one stomach waiting to be filled, while over there they will have thirty-seven stomachs. This means fewer forests and more fields to grow food, and more machinery to produce on this field. They use machinery too, after all, and they will someday drive cars as well.

If at least half of those thirty-seven children drive a car eventually, that will add fourteen compared to the one car of our one child here, which will lead (as it already has profoundly in India and China, for example) to more pollution there too, deterioration of the environment, and eventually increase hunger worldwide.

The solution is if all the governments in the world agree to restrict, not only what is released into the air, water, and soil, but population growth. All religions must join this effort, change their view on population growth. It has to be stopped. Religion and government worldwide have to teach birth control, and everybody has to know that less children is better. Let us do what we are supposed to do, manage the Earth, not mismanage and destroy it!

I'm writing this chapter of my book in 2013; I wrote the above passage in 1992. The world's population now stands at over 7 billion. Most governments have done very little to stop this runaway increase, and religions have done nothing. We are enjoined to stop polluting, to conserve our natural resources. But can any government stop the real cause of global pollution by mere talk?

Two months ago, I caught a follow-up of the show *Born Free*, which was first aired thirty years ago and is about a woman in Kenya nursing some lion cubs that grew up and were like just like cats to her. At that time there were many thousands of lions there. That woman was killed, not by the lions, but by some man because she was protecting the lions. The human population had grown exponentially in her country, and more and more land was being expropriated for crops and housing. The lions were in the way; in 2013, from a population that numbered in the thousands thirty years ago, only two hundred of these great cats remain in Kenya. What a shame.

And how can there be still an argument, especially from all the world's religions, about the increasing efforts at birth control? Are we not destroying God's beautiful creation and creatures? How can we still believe we are the crown of creation if we are acting like a curse by over-populating the globe? The pollution we make, the land we change, and animals we destroy, the gospel of me, me, me and the heck with the planet—are we worthy of surviving?

I don't think God can be pleased with us at all.

THE STOCK MARKET

To WRITE SOMETHING ABOUT the stock market makes me consider a subject I don't want to remember, but I cannot forget how cruel it was. But I can forgive.

I always looked at the stock market as something for somebody else to do. I'm a CD-investing man; I like an annuity. Especially in the '80s and '90s, CDs carried very high rates of interest, not the 0.10, or less, they do now.

So I went to the bank, where a woman invariably gave me good advice, and I eventually had over forty thousand dollars there in a combination CD and annuity—until, one day, she was no longer at the bank; I heard she had quit and joined a brokerage firm.

After a few years, I received a letter from this brokerage firm, with her signature and the invitation for me to come and see her for some stock market investments.

I'd always heard people who had invested in the market telling me how well they were doing. Thinking about that, and how well she had helped me pick the CD, I thought, Well, let's try it with a few hundred dollars, and I went to see her.

My wife and I went. The two women were so happy to see each other again, and that included me too, so I told her, "I have a couple hundred dollars with me to invest."

"Oh, no," she said. "That's not an investment. You need more than that. How about the CD? Cash it in. I know it's time for a renewal. This should be around thirty thousand by now for the stock market, and your annuity's a round twelve. I will it invest in a life insurance policy for you, so your wife is secure if something happens to you." I could see she remembered everything about me and knew exactly what I had in the bank.

I was shocked at this, but she did not let go. She said, "The CD interest will be going down, as you know, and you never know how your annuity will go. I have invested for many people, and including my parents. They are very happy. You will be, too. The market is the future—you will make more money than ever."

So I cashed in the CD and the annuity, about forty-two thousand combined, although the bank warned me not to. She put $12,900.00 into a life insurance "which will always be guaranteed," she said, plus the investment earnings in it, no matter what, and she invested the remaining thirty thousand in in the stock market.

I did not know that the life insurance was put in to stock, too.

All went fine for a few months; the market and the life insurance did make money. Then came whatever it was the market lost, and the insurance, too. "Oh, don't worry, it's only temporary," I was assured. "Just pay our handling fee. It will go up again."

But every time the market report was sent to me, it

was lower, and the handling fee stayed the same.

Finally I had had enough. I had completely liquidated my CD and annuity, and more than half of the proceeds were gone. The insurance was down from $12,900.00 to five thousand. My question was, If I die now, what then?

I was told that it would still be $12,900.00, guaranteed, for my wife to get. Would it be? I hoped so.

Thirty years later, the insurance is still there, not in the stock market any more but in something more secure, I'm promised, and is about seven thousand. I hope my wife will get the $12,900.00 as I'm always promised, not only seven thousand— after all, I'm lot older now.

Just think: The $42,000.00 in the bank would have more than doubled, probably tripled, by now. No wonder my hair's turned gray and white so soon.

It had better be twelve thousand; if not, this woman thinks I will never know because I'll be dead. All this is so on my mind now while I'm alive—I will know what my wife gets when I'm dead too. If it is less than twelve thousand, I will haunt that woman. I will sit on her shoulder and growl in her ears again, and again, "Twelve thousand dollars!" and she will not be able to talk to anybody again; not even a doctor will be able to help her, since my growl will drown all else out. This I promise. She will know from then on, for the rest of her life, that ghosts exist. I just hope there is some room left on her shoulder and not too many ghosts sitting there already, and that they give me some room, too.

THE STORY OF MY LIFE

THE HISTORY OF THE Yugoslav Donau Schwabens (Danube Germans) is my ancestors' first.

Here's the story of the Germans in Yugoslavia, the former Austria/Hungary. Beginning in the late 1600s to the early 1700s, it was part of the Austro-Hungarian Empire. At that time, the German Empress Maria Theresa, with the agreement of Austria, had Germans immigrate into Austrian provinces the way people moved to the West in America.

The land was, at that time, nothing but swamp, bog, and marsh. Nobody lived there; anybody willing to drain the land could have what they drained. Most of the first wave of immigrants expired from all the sicknesses the bog brought with it. The second group was able to get a foothold, however, and survive. These were the ancestors of the Donau Schwabens.

Over the years many new people followed from Serbia, Hungary, and Romania. This land was called Banat, Batschka, and Srem; each was a county or small state—at that time known as a protectorate under Austria/Hungary. Serbia was independent, the only state not under Austro-Hungarian regulations in the region.

At the end of the World War I, Austria lost this land to Serbia. Banat was split up between Serbia and Romania. Batschka and part of Banat (a.k.a., Batschka; see "Vojvodina" on the Internet) each had an independent province go to Serbia. In addition, Serbia got Croatia, Slovenia, Bosnia, and a lot more land from Austria-Hungary, forming a new kingdom to be called "Yugoslavia."

The population of this homeland remained the same, absorbing all the people on the land as it was. The first king of the Kingdom of Yugoslavia, Alexander Karadordevic (from December 1918) was assassinated October 9, 1934. His son Peter succeeded him about two years later as King Peter Karadordevic.

Most of my ancestors (from 1700 on), and I, were born in Werschetz (the German name) (or Vrsac, the Serbian one, these days known as Banat, a town of 32,000 in my time). The natives were of mixed national groups, though I was born on September 5, 1931, of only German descendants.

When I was about three years old, my parents moved to Betchkerek (now called Zrenjanin), which had about 35,000 inhabitants, for business reasons. My father opened a merchandise-moving business, with his own design of specially built large flat-back horse wagons, with automobile-type coil springs, wheel bearings, and rubber wheels with rims and tubes in themas in a car; these were manufactured in town by a carpenter and blacksmith to my father's design. It was something new to them.

This vehicle enabled the horses to pull a much larger load than the then-common smaller regular wagons with bushings on wooden wheels only. That prompted many businesses to have their merchandise delivered to them by my father.

My mother opened a business selling building materials like a Portland cement, sand and lime, plaster, and fertilizer. By 1941, my father had fourteen horses, ten wagons, a big Mercedes truck with a trailer, and a pickup truck for interstate freight transport, with about twenty workers. I went to a German school in town. My sister, Margarete, was born there on March 6, 1937.

The population of Betchkerek was, as I have said, mixed— there were German, Serbian, Hungarian, and Romanian sections, and there were Serbian, Hungarian, and Romanians schools, too.

To be in business, you had to speak more than one language because of the mix of the population. My father spoke all four, my mother and I three—German, Serbian, and Hungarian. My sister was speaking only German and Serbian.

These languages came quite naturally, because we were playing with some Serbian and Hungarian kids, besides Germans. By the time I was five, I had no trouble with Serbian, and by eight I could read it just as well as German, although it was in Cyrillic. By the time I was ten, I had a Hungarian tutor after school. None of the children around us in town spoke only one language, though that was not so in the villages.

Regardless what nationality people were, there was thus a big mix. In villages of only one nationality, however, you had to speak only their language. If it was a Serbian town, you spoke Serbian; in a German one, you spoke German, and so forth. So if you traveled on business, you had to know all the languages.

At the start of World War II, King Peter was on the throne. In 1940, Germany wanted a non-aggressive agreement with Yugoslavia. Yugoslavia refused. (Personally, I saw large groups of several hundred Serbs march in the streets then, shouting, *"Boilje ratt nego pakt!"* ("Better war than a pact").

The German army invaded Yugoslavia around Easter 1941, after non-negotiation, without much resistance from Yugoslavia. King Peter escaped to the United States.

On September 10, 1941, five days after my tenth birthday, my thirty-eight-year-old father, Michael Bader, went on a long business trip to Serbia to buy some building material for my mother's store, as he had done many times (at times I went with him). Such trips typically took two to three days.

This time, Serbian partisans stopped the train and took him off, made him dig his own grave, and then they cut his throat. He was the first German killed in Yugoslavia by Tito's partisans; Tito was the new leader of the Serbian resistance to Germany and all the Germans living in Yugoslavia. So, solely because he was German, my father was murdered. There were many more killings of Germans for the same reason. We had no idea what had happened to my father for two years.

Emilie Bader (thirty-two that time), our mother, searched over the radio, in newspapers, and with the police for those two years without a hint of what had happened to him or where he was—until we were notified by the German government in late 1943, after a confession by one of the partisans involved captured by the German army. By the end of 1941, when my father had not returned, she had taken his business, and, in turn, her mother, assumed my mother's business.

In 1942, all males age sixteen to sixty-five of German descent got drafted into the army, including my mother's brother Anton Breinich (who was thirty-two then), and my father's youngest brother, Joseph Bader (twenty-eight). They went to fight the Partisans, then the Russians, and in Western Europe; many got killed, including Bader. All the Serbians, Hungarians, and Romanians could stay in their homes and continue to do whatever business they had without interference from the German army (though Serbia prosecuted us Germans after the war.)

Beginning in 1944, with the advance of the Russian army against the German army in the war in Yugoslavia, the German army warned all people of German descent living in Yugoslavia to move to Germany. Many of the Germans left all their possessions behind, including houses, farmland, and other property. They left with just a horse-wagon full whatever the horses could pull. Our town was daily blocked by thousands of wagons moving through it. It went on for three months. I don't know how many thousands left. These German people could escape with their "documents of birth and ownership," although they never regained anything they had left behind, or returned home again.

My mother thought about going too—we could have loaded most of our stuff on the truck—but she decided that we would stay. She did not want to give up on her home and business. The Mercedes truck was eventually confiscated by the German army before it left. The rest of the business was left untouched by the Germans, but all was lost anyway to Josiv Brost Tito's partisans after the Russian army came in.

On October 2, 1944, after two days of fighting around us, sitting in the basement of the house, with the cannons of both sides firing over our heads, a German cannon was standing on the corner of the street the house was on, shooting two or three times an hour, for a day. When the truck they were using to move it stopped working, they dynamited it; there was an enormously loud boom, louder than the shots fired before; the truck was almost disintegrated, and the motor truck was propelled through the air and feel through the roof of our house into the attic. The cannon got never removed, and, later in the week, kids played on it.

Our town, Betchkerek, was then invaded, and most of

the German men who had stayed behind in Yugoslavia, those sixty-five or older (all the ones from sixteen to sixty-five had been drafted earlier—there were no younger German men home anymore) got shot and then hung on the gallows to show what happened to the Fascists (the Germans did not get called Nazis by the Russians). I remember, when I was a thirteen-year-old, standing under one of these gallows, which had five men hanging from it with gunshots to their foreheads and the backs of their heads missing. I also heard of two boys younger than sixteen getting shot for just being "German" and out on the street.

In our town on November 6, 1944, the first German women who had not left Yugoslavia got put into a concentration camp. On November 28, the rest of the German women, and children of any age, got interned in the concentration camp in Betchkerek, too. My mother, Emilie Bader (thirty-five), my grandmother, Emma Breinich (fifty-three), Great-Grandmother Maria Scheich (seventy), my sister, Margarete Bader (seven), and I were all interned there.

Whatever you could carry with you on your back, you could take; the rest was all lost. In the large magazine of an oil factory, several thousand of us wound up. We were searched, and all documents, as well as half what we had carried in, got confiscated. From then on, it was as if we did not exist, to Yugoslavia or the world, anymore, so that we would not be able to make any claims against the Yugoslavian government in the future. For the next three days, all we got was so-called "coffee," which was actually much-burned bread ground to powder and then cooked in water into a black liquid.

On the third day, the Serb partisan guards asked all the old women who were ill and unable to work to come forward to be taken to a hospital. About three to four hundred came forward and were marched behind the building and machine gunned in earshot of the rest of us. Then the partisans returned and asked if anyone else needed to go to the hospital. The next day, one of the guards asked me to take my shoes off—they were still new, and he wanted them. I said no.

He put the barrel of his rifle to my forehead in front of everyone.

My grandmother and some women had to hold my mother back when she tried to help me. She would have been killed. I still refused. I looked at him, seeing the barrel of the rifle above my nose, staring into his eyes, and kept that eye-to-eye contact for some time. No words were spoken.

Suddenly he lowered the weapon and retreated. He could have shot me anytime; there would not have been any repercussions for him.

For the next three years, I would be wearing the same shoes. As my feet grew, we cut the top front of the shoes off and held the soles and the rest in place with wires. When we later escaped through Hungry, that's how I walked.

On December 6, 1944, all the women and children in the cooking-oil factory had to go on a fifteen-kilometer march from Betchkerek to a former German village called Katreinfeld; children two years old or younger were loaded onto a dozen or fifteen wagons pulled by horses, and the rest had to walk ahead of them. As some of the women got tired and weaker and collapsed, if they did not get help from the rest of us, they were run over by the wagons and shot thereafter.

It was raining and snowing all the time; to keep everybody going the guards fired their rifles over our heads continuously and, from time to time, violently threw a hand grenade as far as they could. Whether anybody was injured by those grenades, I don't know, but the explosions were loud enough to hurt your ears.

In Katreinfeld, we had to spend the night in a schoolyard, sitting on our sacks, freezing. In the morning, some of the older women (including my great-grandmother) were separated from the rest of us. They stayed behind, while we were marched eight kilometers to Kleck, another small village of about 250 houses, owned by German farming families. These houses had been given to new Serbian owners. Only, on the outskirts of the town, there was a street of about fifty houses of Romanians.

We were put into the gym of school building (about five to six hundred people lying on the floor, on straw, in rows, next to each other—women and children. (This was sleeping accommodation for duration in Kleck for almost a year.) We had no heat, no water, and no food that day. There was never any heat that winter.

The next day, the guards formed details—how many should go for ration of cornmeal to the commandant for all interned, then cook it in a big kettledrum, with no salt, sugar, or spices ever added. Others had to go for water, which needed to be carried in water cans from a pump off the corner at the end of street. The rest of us had to go into the fields to harvest whatever was possible.

The surrounding fields had, as I've said, been owned by Germans. Just as in other towns, almost all of the Germans had abandoned those houses and fields, loaded their wagons with what valuable possession could be transported, and fled to Germany from the Russian army. The fields had not, therefore, been harvested. So the corn, the grain, and what else was left was harvested in the middle of the winter.

The women were under guard all day out there, frozen, wet, and hungry, a slice of cornbread when they got back (they got a ration of about a cup of cornmeal and this was it, every day). My mother had to go in the kitchen with two other women, under guard, to cook for the eighty-eight guards, but were never allowed to eat anything; and I, with another boy, Jochan Dasinger, who was a year older than I, had to split and cut wood for this kitchen. Some girls eleven to thirteen years old had to peel potatoes, carrots, and what else had to be cooked. But we were not allowed to eat any of the cooked food—only our ration of corn meal at the camp.

I had to start work at 4:00 a.m. and continue until 6:00 or 8:00 p.m.

Sometime in March, a group of Soviet officers came to the camp. We had to go past them in a single line, and one just pointed with his thumb to the right or left. All the young women who looked fairly healthy went to the right, and the children and older women to the left. The right side was marched to the train and shipped to Russia, to work there digging in coalmine labor camps. My mother had an infected leg that saved her. Any children of those women, no matter how young, baby or older, stayed behind and had to be cared for by the rest of us, relative or not.

That summer, Dasinger and I had to go for water for the kitchen. We passed a pond with the water in it almost evaporated. In the pond we found a hand grenade tossed in during the war (there was a lot of war matériel lying around all over). We took the grenade—Dasinger said he wanted the fuse out of it.

When we were back with the water, he started to try to open it up, and his seven-year-old brother came to see what we were doing. I got scared when he started to hammer on the thing, and walked away with the brother. We were about fifty meters away from him when the grenade went off. We dove to the ground, and I looked in Dasinger's direction. A big cloud of smoke was covering him. He was still standing. Then he moaned, and I could see he had lost an arm and a foot. His right side was completely mangled. How he was still up standing on that one foot, I don't know. Then he collapsed. The guards came running and shot him. His brother was wounded slightly on the ear. I had no wounds, but the biggest shock of my life ever.

The next day, I had to scrape pieces of his flesh from the nearby wall that had splattered on it and were sticking to it like ground hamburger. The birds were there for two days picking pieces off the ground.

We were in Kleck almost a year—most the time, day and night, in the same clothes. There was no water for washing. We washed only sometimes in the summer. I know this you think this is impossible, but it is true. And it got worse—much worse.

In the beginning, around October 1945, all of us were transported from Kleck to Rudolfgnad, a village of around five thousand German people, mostly farmers who had fled before World War II ended.

There were about 450 houses in town. The average house had a kitchen and two to three rooms, and they were all built of brick. They had a large backyard for chicken, a pigsty, and corrals for horses.

All the livestock was, of course, gone. Only straw from weed-stalks of many acres of weed compressed together to a size three times that of the house for bedding of the animals lay in each back yard.

This was also our bedding, spread on the floor

through the house, and the only source for heating. The houses also all had a big oven built into a wall, which was filled with straw; heat from one filling of this oven lasted one night in the winter. Many days, nobody was able to fill it, and the house got so cold that, in the morning, the water in cups was frozen.

This town was encircled by an eight-foot-high barbed-wire face, and about thirty thousand Germans, from different camps in different towns of Banat, got concentrated in this one. This concentration camp turned into a death camp for thousands of Germans dying from starvation and sickness.

When we got there, my great-grandmother, whom we had had to leave behind in Katreinfeld, was already there, and, from the camp of the town of Werschetz, the two children my mother's brother Anton Breinich, the son Alfred Breinich (seven then) and his sister Helga (who was one and a half), my two cousins, with their grandmother in a different house. The mother, Hedwick Breinich (my aunt), had been shipped to Russia working in the coal mines and did not survive. Where my uncle was, we did not know. How my mother found the children, I don't know either, but she took them into the house we were in, and Helga started to call my mother "mom."

The house we were in had a kitchen and two rooms. There were between sixty and seventy people in each house, a mix of children, some just months old, and women up to in their eighties, all from many towns put into one.

We still had the same food, cornmeal, never any salt or sugar or any type of fat, and on some days just nothing—especially on Christmas or holidays, one day we burst the seal on the attic door and found a chamber full of dried peas (a life saver).

Sicknesses, not enough food, no doctors, no medication—not even an aspirin—or sugar, or salt, killed hundreds of people every day in the camp.

By January, almost all the people in all the houses were ill. I was having a problem around my knees and elbows—no more skin—and I could not sit up without it turning black in front of my eyes from malnutrition. I was lying next to my great-grandmother. When my grandmother and some other women carried me to another place in the house I did not know, but my great-grandmother died next to me on January 27, 1946, her seventy-second birthday. Shortly after that, Helga died, too. Her last words were to my mother: "Mom, I will go now to my real mom," she said. She was two years old.

Death came nearly every day that winter. I had a dead woman above my head who lay there for more than a day because nobody was able to move her. As the clothes of the survivors got damaged, the dead bodies got stripped of their clothes if they were in better shape, and the dead simply got put outside by whoever was strong enough.

Some wagons, pulled by horses, stopped by each house, and the dead got thrown on them, up to thirty per wagon. There was a mass grave—a ditch the length of a football field—and the bodies were just thrown in, up to five layers high, hundreds of them. They poured powdered limestone over them, then bulldozed it shut.

Every day, not to have my arms and legs glue together at the wounds—I had no skin on my arms and legs around the elbows and knees any more, and something was leaking out of the wounds —two women ripped me apart; sometime, my grandmother helped, because my mother was too ill.

Pain—well! And the stuff oozed through all my clothes, which never got washed and stuck to me. Many other children and grown-ups had all kinds of infections, too. Some survived, some not; there was no doctor around. Some women brewed tea from all kinds of plants growing around the houses. The handful of dried peas now and then was full of bugs, but we ate them just as well, hundreds of them. They crunched and crackled between your teeth. Oh yes, when you are hungry, you eat everything, even worms and beetles, frogs and birds we could catch. I survived; luckily, the winter was short.

In the spring, somewhere between eighteen hundred and two thousand kids, eight years and older, had to go at 6:00 in the morning to report to the guards and go for a fifteen-to-seventeen-kilometer round trip in the woods to gather two bundles of branches, one for the guards' kitchen, and one to carry home at night for the house they were in.

By that time I had recuperated some, and I got included, too. We walked this mostly barefoot; the dust we created choked the last ones in the column quite badly, and there was no water to drink all day unless we got close to a brook. Weak as I still was, I was one of them; the thirst was sometimes overpowering, even the hunger we felt. (To this day I still don't need too much water—I'm always reminded by my wife to drink more.)

This went on every day for months, till I had to go plowing in the field with horses. All the women still able to had to work in the fields, too. This was hard work, but at least you could sneak some berries or other food, though it had to be so no guard saw it; if you got caught, you got beat up or put in the cellar at the guard station, which was chest high and filled with water, so you could not sit down, sometimes for two days. Many did not get out alive.

I was caught with a still-green apple from a tree we passed going to work; right from behind, a guard sneaked up and hit me on my head with a walking stick. Believe me, I could hear the bells from the bell tower in London ringing. And the apple turned in to a big headache, but at least I was not thrown in the cellar.

In March 1947, my mother was called in to the commandant of the camp. He asked her for her name. When he heard "Bader," he asked if she knew an Anton Bader. "Yes," she said. "That's my brother in-law."

My uncle, I never learned how, had found us and gotten in touch with the commandant. My uncle had a grain-processing business in Yugoslavia dealing with all kinds of grains. He had nine carts with people driving around to buy grains, corn, and other farm products from farmers, which he sold in big shipments to other European countries. This made him well-known, and it turned out the commandant knew him because he was one of his employees earlier. The Partisans had been ready to shoot my uncle then but somehow changed their minds and let him go. He escaped to Salzburg Austria in his car. This is of course another story.

The commandant said to my mother, "I give you a break," and put my family—mother, grandmother, my sister, cousin, and me—on the train with a guard. We got shipped to Gakovo in the province of the Batschka, also a town with concentration camp, but one that has no fence around it. To our surprise, we found my grandmother and grandfather, Katarina and Joseph Bader, there. They were in another house but close by. The daily food was still cornbread, but it was already baked, and there was a pond, to my surprise, full of frogs. We did not have to do any kind of work, so we had a lot of frog's legs to eat because nobody else ate them, and there was much less control of what you did, so stuff like this was easier to come by without punishment.

When we came upon my grandfather for the first time, it was a big surprise; we'd had no idea of what had happened to them. My grandfather informed us that Gakovo was only seven kilometers from the Hungarian border, and that, at night, people always tried—many successfully—to cross to Hungary, but it was risky: People sometimes got shot or punished when caught.

It started to dawn on us why we had been moved to Gakovo.

Around the beginning of August the family decided that we would risk it, and, after receiving some information from Gakovo inhabitants how to go, we left in the night. My grandfather and the two grandmothers stayed behind.

We had walked about two kilometers when there was some commotion ahead of us. We huddled down. Then, suddenly, some guard start shooting. My cousin and I stumbled in a ditch; where my mother and sister had gone, we did not know.

The bullets came so close that the top of the ditch we were in got hit and sprayed us with dirt. The night was very dark, and after the shooting stopped, I and my cousin just stayed there.

Suddenly my mother and sister—they were OK, too—found us again. How she was able to do this, I don't know. We started to move again but, maybe a kilometer short of the border, we got caught by some guard.

They did not turn us back but took us to the border, where several other people from the camp who had been caught were being held. The guards interrogated us; my mother, speaking Serbian, told them where we wanted to go.

They decided to let us go and handed us over to the Hungarian border guards. Most likely this was some kind of a deal. The Hungarians took us to a big cornfield, and then disappeared.

They let all the Germans go, and we all spread into the field because we were not confident that we would not get killed if we didn't.

We never saw anyone from that group again; we were on our own.

The trip though Hungary was spent day and night in the fields. From time to time my cousin, my sister, and I went begging in Hungarian for something to eat. Most the time we did get something, but at times we had to run, too.

After a couple of days we passed a town. At the end of a street stood a truck with some men talking nearby. My mother approached and talked to them. After a while, one of them signaled to come. He was the driver. My mother and sister could sit in the cab, and my cousin and I climbed onto the back of the truck. It happened that the driver had to go to a town in the direction of the Austrian border, and that saved us, thanks to my mother's ability to speak Hungarian, a couple of weeks of walking. And he gave her some advice about how to continue too, but we were still far from the border and soon on our own again.

After a few days walking we got stopped at a police

control point. They marched us for two hours to a train station in the next town. We got loaded on a railroad train that traveled for hours and stopped at many stations. We were not entirely sure where we were going.

Then another guard took us off the train. He marched us into a big yard where there were already maybe a hundred people like us, refugee Germans from Yugoslavia. They told us at night that we would be turned over to the Austrians, which they did.

Austrian guards took us to a big building were we had to wait till the morning. In the morning we were informed that we were in the Russian zone.

They asked my mother where she wanted to go. After she said, "Salzburg," she was told that Austria had been divided into four zones—Russian, French, English, and American. To cross a zone without official documents verboten (not allowed) at that time; it was it was like crossing a border. Salzburg was in the American zone.

So we had to stay in the Russian zone. She had to find work there. She applied, and I applied too, when she heard of a farmer looking for workers near the English zone, which was between the Russian and the American.

Again we got loaded onto a train and told to get off at a certain town (I don't remember the name), and that a farmer would be there. When the train pulled in, we got off, but on the other side of the train, and started to run into the field, where we hid in some bushes; after the train left and we were sure that nobody was looking for us, we started to walk again.

In the evening, just before night, we reached a narrow river, on the other side of which was the English zone. It was not officially permitted to cross it without papers, nor were we sure how deep it was or whether there were guards on the other side, so we waited for night to fall.

Just then a few cows came from the field and started to cross the river. If they did not swim, we realized, the river could not be too deep. My mother pushed us among them, and that was the way we got across the river, hidden by the cows.

The next day, we reported to the Austrian police.

Again we were put in camp with other refugees for six weeks, to be checked for illnesses and to try to find some relatives. They informed my uncle Bader of our whereabouts. He wrote us that he would come and get us when the six-week internment ended. (My sixteenth birthday, on September 5, 1947, took place in that camp.)

To our surprise my mother's brother's uncle, Anton Breinich, the father of my cousin Fredi, showed up to get his family and my mother, sister and me. The bad news for him was that his wife and little girl were dead. Till then, he had not known what happened to them. He was an American prisoner of war at the end of the war and set free in Salzburg, where my uncle Bader had immigrated, too. Their meeting in Salzburg was a surprise to them both.

He had to go from the English zone, sneaking in to the

American zone, to free us after the six weeks. After a train ride of several hours, we got close to the American zone. Again we got off the train, walking endlessly to the American zone, then sneaking at night over into it.

We had been trudging along for about an hour in the American zone when a military policeman in uniform, and a civilian, came by in a Jeep (at that time, a General Motors product) and stopped us. He was talking English; my uncle shook his head and said, "*Ich kann nichts ferstehen*" ("I cannot understand"). The civilian was Austrian and worked as a translator; after we told him we were looking for work in the next town, the American let us go.

It was my first encounter with an American and a Jeep automobile.

So we were finally in the American zone. The next day, we took a train to Salzburg, and a new life began.

Uncle Breinich worked for a construction company that was canalizing Salzburg City. He had a room at the company, and we moved in with him. Here my uncle was, a man who had owned a big clothing store in Werschetz, now lining up and laying six-foot-diameter canal pipes in the ground every day.

My mother started to work for the same construction company, in the office, eight hours with four to six hours a day of overtime to make money. My sister and my cousin started to go to school. They were both ten years old, and going to the first grade was hard for them because of their age, but they made two years in one for a few years and caught up.

I started to learn automobile mechanics, which consisted of working four days in the garage, and spending one day in school, each week. This went on for four and a half years; then I had a two-day test in order to become a journeyman in automobile repair. It was the requirement for becoming an auto mechanic.

The same rule applied to any trade, whether you were a hair dresser or a tailor or whatever—you took a test after four and a half years.

Uncle Anton Bader married a girl from Salzburg and opened a business, then got some stock money from AEG, a German company he had invested in while still in Yugoslavia, relocated to Germany, and built a house and business there.

In the meantime, my grandfather Joseph Bader died in the concentration camp in Gakovo at the end of 1947, and my two grandmothers were finally, a year and a half later in 1948, released from the camp. After another year and a half, we are able to get permission for them to come to Austria and Germany from Yugoslavia. My mother's mother, Emma Breinich, came to us in to Salzburg, and my father's mother, Katrina Bader, to my uncle Bader in Germany.

In Salzburg I joined a group of "Folks Deutche or Donau Swaben" (that's what we were called by the Austrians, meaning immigrants of German folks). We got together once a week—all young girls and boys of my age, to sing and dance traditional dances of the Yugoslavian Germans. We got so good that we were invited to perform in several cities in Germany and Austria.

After a few years, a girl named Anna Seidl, a German from Filipovo, Yugoslavia, joined the group and got to be my dance partner, and, in April 1955, we married; I was twenty-four, my wife nineteen.

The Seidl Family had a house in Filipovo, in the Batschka region of Yugoslavia. Filipovo was a village of several thousand Germans. Her father, Franz Seidl, had gotten drafted in 1942 by the Germans. The rest of the family was interned in 1945 in the concentration camp in Gakovo—Anna's mother, Gertrude Seidl (forty, née Sendelbach) and children Katie (nineteen), Hans (seventeen), Franz (thirteen), Magdalena (eleven), Anna (nine), Richard (seven), Adolf (five), and Gerda(two). There my wife lost her mother, her brother Richard, and the sister Gerda. They were starved just as badly as we were in Rudolfgnad. (I did not know Anna in Gakovo.) The family was split up—Katie, Hans, and Franz got interned in concentration work/camps but survived; so did Leni, Anna, and Adolf.

Anna and some of her family did also, and after several years they came to Salzburg.

Her father, after five years in a Russian prisoner-of-war camp, was released in 1949 to Yugoslavia, and from there was able to come to Salzburg, where he was reunited with his family. When he left 1942, he'd had a wife and eight children; seven years later, he had no wife and only six children left.

I passed my test and worked for about an additional year in the garage. In 1952, my boss was upset when I left and went to work for the American army, repairing Jeeps and REO trucks. When Austria regained its independent three years later, the four occupying military powers left—shortly after I had married—and I had to get new employment, which I found in a motorcycle factory. I did not want to go back to a garage because I got better pay in the factory. On March 5, 1956, my first daughter, Hannelore, was born.

The motorcycle factory made arrangements to move to Vienna, which meant I would lose my job again. I applied then to immigrate to the United States. At the time, you needed a sponsor to promise you'd have work when you arrived. My wife had an uncle in Jeffersonville, New York, who had immigrated there three years before. We asked him if he could get a sponsor, and he got a chicken farmer to do it.

On November 15, 1956, with the grieving of the rest of the family, especially of my mother and grandmother and my wife's father and family, my wife and baby daughter (eight months old then) left with the help of a Catholic agency on an airplane bound for New York City with about eighty other immigrants. I had $95.00 in my pocket. That was the last time I saw both grandmothers and my uncle Bader alive; they died in the beginning of the sixties.

In 1956, my sister married Anton Vogel, also a German from Yugoslavia, and they immigrated, with a baby girl, to Australia, after which my mother and grandmother were, regrettably, alone.

Our second daughter, Christina, was born in June 1957, in the Hospital of Liberty. A little later, I started to work at the Ford plant in Mahwah. Our third daughter, Irene, followed in June 1958—also in Liberty. Our son, Michael, was born in February 1960, in Suffern, New York; we were living by then in Ramapo, in Rockland County, New York. We bought our house in Mahwah, in New Jersey's Bergen County, in 1961.

In 1972 my wife, I, and Hannelore became citizens of the United States. In 2004, we lost Hannelore to an illness; we miss her continually.

On June 30, 1980, the assembly plant of the Ford Motor Company in Mahwah closed, and—you guessed it—I suddenly had no job again after twenty-three years plus. I could have transferred to another plant, but it was too far away to drive every day, and I didn't want to relocate.

All four children went to college—Hannelore for computing, Christina for nursing, Irene for accounting, and Michael for chemistry and business.

In August 1980, when Christina was working as a registered nurse in a Bergen County hospital, she told me that they were looking for somebody to repair washers in the laundry.

I had built a forty-two-by-sixteen-foot addition to my home, mostly by myself with the help of my wife; I had fixed many appliances for us and the neighbors—even some fourteen- to-sixteen-pound-load washing-machine units. I was sure I knew how to repair washing machines, so I applied.

When they took me down to the laundry, I found that the smallest washer had an eighty-five-pound load, another five-hundred, and two seven-hundred. They washed a load in forty-five minutes and were immediately reloaded and run again, all day long. There were Dryers, lint collectors, two sheet folders, a small apparel folder, three air compressors, and a lot more—you get the idea. I had never been in a laundry before, so I was stumped. When I was asked if I could repair those machines, my taught was, I have no job now, so what could happen? If I get fired, I'll be in the same position, so I said, "Sure." And, yes, I was the only repair man there.

How I managed to stay in the laundry is another story. Those machines had thousands of parts I hadn't known existed before. But the laundry manager realized I was a quick learner and good worker, and helped me to manage. For a year I was standing in front of the machines and studying what went on when they were running and how to repair them—many times on my own time. Five years later I was included in the purchase of another laundry machine in Pennsylvania; it was nineteen feet high, reaching into the upper floor, and was fifty-four feet long. When loaded, it could wash a 110 pounds of laundry every three minutes, and dry them. In 1992, after twelve years, I retired. I've been retired longer than I worked at any of my jobs in the U.S.A.

At eighty-two, I figure the ending to my story will have to be written by somebody else. Whoever does it will be able to make use of a family tree a great-uncle gave to our mother in Austria.

SUN AND DAUGHTER

THE OTHER DAY, I started thinking why a boy is called
a son and a girl a daughter—where did these names
come from?

When humans started to talk and the language started
to develop, it was in primitive times, and "son" must have
come from the Sun, because they could see it daily it was
the biggest object in the sky. So since a male child was
special, it got the name of the Sun. "Son" sounds equally
important.

But how did the word "Daughter" come to be?

There was nothing that sounded like "doter "or "daughter" in the sky. There were stars, many of them, but they
were too small and not worthy of a girl's name, I would say.
They could have called a girl "Starlet," but then there were
no movies then.

However, there was a Moon. How come they did not
call a daughter "moona"? After all, the moon was, to the
wisdom of that time, the second-biggest object in the sky.
Logic would seem to dictate that "moona"would be about
right. If no, would "mooney" have been better?

I put my daughter Christina to the test on my driveway one day and asked her how "moona"would sound to

her instead of "daughter"? She looked at me so strangely, I expected she was going to send me to a doctor. So I had to explain my reasoning.

The look of rejection increased tenfold, and if those looks had been hot coals, I would have been burned to ashes (which would have saved some money, because I would not have had to be cremated any more).

Then she got her wits back. "Oh, no," she said. "A daughter is much bigger than the Sun, you know! She will eventually be a Milky Way." She turned to her car and left me standing there.

And I thought, Moona! I thought I'd hit on something!" Milky-Way" instead of "daughter" would never have come to my mind—this is absolutely a big *whoa*.

Which only goes to show how women are smarter. "Milky-Way!" I have to get over this—just how?

THE TICKET

L AST SUNDAY I TURNED right from 17 North onto a small street in Ramsey to shop at the Pathmark supermarket. After I had shopped, to get back to route 17 North I have to drive through the parking lot, around the supermarket and some stores in a big building, make a left turn, cross four lanes of highway, drive to a light, wait for it to turn green, make another left turn, and drive down the same short street, this time in the other direction, so I can drive home to Mahwah. It's just as confusing as it sounds.

There's a much shorter way if I go back to the entrance where I came into the supermarket parking lot, then cross the street, make a left turn, drive down the same short street that I traveled after the turn at the light, and get onto 17 north.

So why all this driving around the store, and not go the shorter way? There's a good reason: There's a *No Left Turn* sign there, but it was Sunday and I did not want to waste time going around the supermarket, and since there were no cars coming in any direction, I made this illegal turn.

I went across and had just made my left turn onto the short street when, from nowhere, a police car appeared behind me with the red lights on. There must be an emergency somewhere, I thought. I moved to the right so he could pass me, but he stopped too—behind me!

He'd had the gall to hide behind some bushes—and this on a Sunday? How come he wasn't in church?

"License, registration, and insurance card, please."

At that moment, I knew I'd had it, and handed the documents to him. He disappeared into his car and, when he came back, he very politely handed me an eighty-six-dollar ticket with two points on my license and asked, "Why did you make this illegal turn?"

"Because I was stupid," I said—how much grocery could I have bought for eighty-six bucks?

He said, "Thank you for your honesty."

This made me wonder—had he just insulted me, and was he thinking I was stupid all the time? Or had I been stupid just this time?

Maybe he was right—I was doubly stupid, first to make the turn, and second to admit that I was stupid instead of saying, "Oh, please, Officer, don't stick your head in the window—I have to go home so badly to go the toilet. I stink! Please let me go. You can follow me, and when I leave the toilet I'll give you what you asked for." (Is it not true that good ideas always come too late? That would've gotten me off.

But what then if he'd have stuck his nose into the car

to verify what I was claiming? Would I have had to cover up by going into my pants, just to tell the truth? Or would he have accepted and followed me home? Or given me another ticket for insulting an officer. It is so hard to make my mind up whether I'm stupid or maybe just look it.

Of course, I have to pay the ticket either way.

THE WEATHER REPORTERS
BEFORE TV

ONCE, GRANDMA OR GRANDPA reported the weather. When the arthritis pain acted up, it was a "rainy day coming," and they were generally accurate.

Then came TV with its learned meteorology, the computers and instruments. Who's better at reporting the weather?

The young new meteorologist is preparing his weather report. He checks all his computers and weather models, and all points to a nice day, all sunshine.

He tells his boss,"On the news, I will forecast a good day with a lot of sunshine."

The boss tells him, "No. Tell them there'll be bad weather and rain."

Stumped, he goes back to the computer and the instruments at the weather stations, the computer reports, and they all tell him there'll be sun out and a good day.

So he goes returns to the boss and says, "All the instruments and computer models call for sunshine, a good day. Why do you want me to say it's going to rain?"

"Forget all that. The big toe on my left foot hurts badly."

The boss turns out to be right, too.

If I would be young a person now and just starting a professional life, I would be a weather reporter, because it doesn't makes any difference what you report. If you say rain and the sun shines, or sunshine and it rains, you don't worry; you can always point out that the sun's shining somewhere else, and so is it with rain. They pay you anyway. It's is the only occupation where you can't be wrong, get fired, and you have a secure job. How much better can it get?

Especially if you listen to your toes.

THIS WAS JOE

THERE WAS A TIME, my darlings, when there were no cell phones. If you needed to reach someone, there were phone booths everywhere into which you could slip (later, they became stands rather than booths) to make your call. On these public telephones in 1970, we all knew that, if there was no connection if you called somebody, the money you put in the phone was returned to you in the return slot. Many of us developed the habit of checking these slots to see if someone had forgotten to retrieve their dime or quarter or more. To some people, this checking grew into an obsession, a sickness.

I knew just such a person.

When I worked in the Ford plant in Mahwah, which employed about five thousand people, there were about twenty in my group. One of them was a fellow named Joe. If he found a coin in a telephone slot, it made his day. In the entrance hall to the plant, there were several public phones, and every break and lunch time, Joe went to check all of them.

One day I had an idea. I told Jim to stall Joe until I gave him a prearranged signal.

At lunch time, I filled the return slot of one of the phones with loose change. I took the phone off the hook, dropped another three dollars' worth of coins in the deposit slot, but did not dial or hang up the receiver. Then I signaled Jim.

When Jim and Joe were close enough, with the phone in my hand, I started to empty the return slot. "Whee! Look at that!" I exclaimed.

Joe heard me emptying the coins out, like a hungry tiger after prey, jumped to my side. "What did you do? What happened? How much is it?"

"Well," I said, "I put in a dime" (that's what a local call cost then—long distance calls were more, depending on the distance), "called my wife, it was busy. . .and all this money came back. I'll try again."

Since I'd never hung up the phone, the coins I had deposited were still in it. I added a dime and dialed the number less one digit, so I never got a connection. After pretending to listen, I hung up, and the three dollars I had deposited before were returned. It sounded like a casino jack-pot. Very calmly, I said, "Still busy!"

Poor Joe—he lost all control. "Did you hear that? What's the matter with you? You don't want the money?" He tried to push me out of his way.

"Hold your horses, Joe," I said. "I heard it. The phone must be broken, and it's not my money but the telephone company's. I'll return it to them."

I emptied the slot again and added the coins to the

ones which I'd taken of the slot earlier, which were sitting on the shelf in front of the phone. It made a nice little pile, and I counted six dollars.

If you ever saw a person utterly speechless, that was Joe. His mouth opened and closed. He inhaled so much air, his chest expanded so much that it looked like he had lost inches in height. Finally it came out: "Are you crazy?" He started moving around with his arms thrashing the air like windmills. "Get out of the way! This is my machine now."

Jim, afraid that Joe was going to attack me, grabbed him from behind. "Let me go. I have to call my wife," Joe shouted. "I always use only this machine. This is my phone...."

Figuring the joke had gone on long enough, I took my money and offered him the phone. He put in a dime, dialed, and hung up. Only the dime was returned. Somewhat calmer, he said, "How come it didn't work for me?"

Realizing that the joke could go on, Jim said, "You didn't wait long enough. Let it ring a few times." In went the dime again, dialing, ringing—and his wife answered.

"Hey," he said, "you cost me money. Hang up, and when you hear a ring, don't pick up the phone." She said something. Joe, now more excited, said, "Listen, when it rings, just don't pick up the phone, OK?"

He hung up. Another dime, dialing, some ringing, hanging up—and only the dime returned. Jim was red as a lobster from holding back his laughter, and I was massaging my face to keep it straight.

Joe looked at us and asked, "Now what? I did all *you* did, and I got only my dime back."

"No, you did not," I told him. "Here's what I did. I dialed my number, and it was busy, and that's how I got the money. You dialed your number."

Since he knew my number, in went a dime, dialing, ringing, and my wife answered. Without a word, he handed me the phone and left. I could not talk to my wife, because Jim and I were laughing so hard we got hysterical; I had to hang up.

When I came home from work, she complained about the funny phone call. Somebody had first breathed heavily, she said, then started laughing like crazy.

After I told her the story, she was breathing heavily too and laughing like crazy.

TODAY'S TOYS

MY FIRST GRANDDAUGHTER HAS one of those talking A.G. bears sitting on her bed. When I pass her bedroom, the noise of my footsteps makes him grumble. Sometimes I stick my head into the room and say, "Hi, A.G.!" Normally the bear repeats what's said. Not with me; he answers, "I love you."

"That's nice," I say, or, "I love you, too."

He replies, "I'm hungry."

I watch enough TV to see some of these horror shows where some of the stuffed animals attack the owner and do deadly things to them. Is not this bear talking already, telling me he loves me just to keep me calm, and, in the next breath, let me know he's hungry? . . . Silly me—the bear is only a decoration.

On the other hand maybe my granddaughter doesn't want me in her bedroom. Teenagers can be tricky; maybe she knows something I don't, and that's why the bear is there. Doesn't the radio sometimes play with nobody in the room? And the lights are on sometimes. . . ? And when I ask, "Why are the lights on?" nobody knows why, or who turned them on. Spooky, spooky. I'd better get going, just in case. "Got to go, A.G.," I tell the bear as I leave.

I hear him say, "I want to hold and hug you."

He never said that before. Sounds dangerous.

Another day, I watched my grandson, a little over two years old, playing on some kind of contraption that has a base standing on the floor. A top platform was turning on ball bearings, with the bearings anchored to the base.

The whole thing was about five inches high. My grandson's stomach was on the top platform, his feet and head stretched straight out and, pushing on the floor with his hands, he twirled himself around and around.

"Hey, that is neat," I said to him. "Where did you get this gadget from?"

"From Santa Claus at Christmas!" he replied.

My mind started to wander back to the time when I had fun spinning with outstretched arms turning around and around, or sitting on a swing, twirling the two ropes together until it almost broke, then lifting my feet up and letting it spin out again.

Suddenly, I had the urge to be small again. "Will you let me spin, too?" I asked.

"Grandpa, you're too fat."

Now, wait a minute, I thought. I know his vocabulary is very good, even at his age. But does his eyesight have to be too? I'd better lose weight. "No, I'm not," I said, and to prove it, I put my hand on the top platform and pushed down. It turned effortlessly. So I put one knee on it, then the other, and it took my weight. "You see? I'm not too fat," I told him. But as soon as I put my stomach on the top platform, the whole contraption disappeared under me. Maybe I was a little too fat after all, but I got some plywood out of the cellar, positioned the toy on the top platform, and, with a little juggling, I was able to do what my grandson did.

I circled one time around, and a second—whoopee, this was fun. After about ten times, I heard my grandson asking, "Grandpa, when is it my turn again?" So I stopped, pushed my plywood off, got up, took one step, and was sitting on the floor again.

I knew I was not on the platform anymore, but the whole house was sitting on it; wherever I looked, everything was spinning. "Is it my turn now?" my grandson asked again.

"Yes, Yes, go ahead. I have to figure out how to get to my chair, because it is still running away from me," I told him. I guess that was the last spin I took; the urge for it was gone. Spinning is for the young. At my age, it gets to be nothing but a run-around.

The other day my second granddaughter (who's five) came to me with a baby doll and a bottle, filled with water, belonging to it. "Grandpy—"she always calls me *Grandpy* if she wants to soap me up for something— "Grandpy, would you please nurse my baby for me?"

I'm the father of four children, but I must admit I did not do that much of the bottle feeding myself; this was a job I somehow never got around to. Now my grand-daughter wants me to feed a doll? My first impulse was, Don't bother me, I have to read the newspaper. Then I looked into her eyes and my hand went for the doll.

The doll had a kind of cute face with an open hole in her mouth and was dressed like a baby. So to go along with the game I said, "Coo-chi-coo, coo-chi-coo, little baby," laid the doll in my arm, and stuck the bottle filled with water in her mouth. A peek at my granddaughter showed me she was really impressed with my parenting ability. The water, about four ounces, was flowing out of the bottle into the doll.

This impressed me; I wondered where all of it was going. It did not take long before I could feel something suspicious happen on my lap, and there was my answer. What goes in must come out. "Oops, I forgot to put a di-aper on her," my granddaughter said with a twinkle in her eyes. She ran for a diaper while I was left with a leaky doll, looking where to press my finger to stop the water flow.

I wonder why the manufacturer of the doll did not suggest pea soup. This would make the whole affair with the doll even more realistic. I must say, these toys drive me. . .or maybe I like them.

TOO MANY RAISINS?

A FTER SECOND GRADE, MY parents used to send sent me "home" to my maternal (Breinich) grandmother during school recess. I put quote marks around "home" because, a few years earlier, for business reasons, my parents had moved to a different town. For me no matter how long I lived in this town, home was the town I had been born in, where all the relatives lived.

My grandfather died a few years earlier, so my grandmother was "thrilled" to have me as her "company," for a few days anyway. But did the thrill last for the whole recess? I would like to believe that it did. Come to think of it, why, did Grandma send me for the raisins? Perhaps the "thrill" was not so everlasting after all.

After a couple of weeks of being the man in the house, my grandmother suggested that I go to my other grandmother's, the mother of my father, to get half a kilogram of raisins. "Grandma, why do you want me to go for raisins? I know where some are." With that I opened a kitchen cabinet and showed her the bag with the raisins in it. I'd found them before, and because I really liked them, I'd sneaked some now and then. It had started to show—the bag had gotten smaller and smaller.

"I want to bake something, and this is not enough," she said.

My fraternal (Bader) grandmother lived on the outskirts of the town; it was more than a two-mile walk. I was not too thrilled to go, but Grandma said, "On the way home, you can have a few raisins." This made it easier for me to go and was a relief for her, too. She'd have at least four hours of peace.

I loved both grandmothers, but for whatever reason—I don't know—I was more comfortable at my maternal grandma's house. So after a couple of hours with my other one, I was ready to walk back. With a good-sized paper bag of raisins in my hand, and also the go-ahead, "You can eat some," I was soon on my way again. I'm sure she was relieved also when I left.

As a good boy, I had to listen to my grandma, didn't I? So I ate some raisins, always squeezing the top of the bag to see if it already showed that some were missing. When it started to, I remembered the other grandma had also said that I could eat some. And, good boy that I was, I had listen to both my grandmas.

When the bag was half empty, I wondered if grandma back "at home" actually knew how much there had been in the bag to begin with. No way! I concluded. So some more raisins went into my stomach. When I squeezed the top of the bag then, I knew I was in trouble—I had to stop.

After walking a block or so, I could not resist. Only one more raisin: Believe me, it was not my fault that six or seven got stuck to my fingers every time I reached into the bag. The bag got smaller and smaller—just "magic," that's all, so, since I was in trouble anyway. . .how much more could I get into if I ate two, or maybe four, more?

By the time I got home, the bag was empty, and I did not feel so hot mentally or physically. Holding the bag behind my back so she could not see that it was empty, I told my grandmother, "I'm home safe, and there's nothing to worry about—everything is alright." She asked me for the raisins, and I had to hand her the bag. To my surprise, the expression on her face did not change. She turned the bag over, and exactly nine raisins fell out.

"How many raisins were in the bag when you left?" she asked me in a very calm voice.

I grabbed the bag and circled it with my fingers quite far down. Then, for some uncontrollable reason, the hand slowly slid farther and farther up, to stop almost at the top of the bag.

"Oh, my God—you ate them all?" The calm voice and expression on her face now were gone. I did not have to answer; a loud growl came deep from my stomach.

To cut the story short, I was a good customer for the toilet for the next two days. For a while, I was even cured of eating raisins after this, but only for a little while. That evening, a good friend of my grandma came to visit. After she left the toilet, she said to my grandmother, "I don't know—your toilet smells like a winery."

"I know,"my grandmother answered. "The wine bottle is right in his bed, if I just knew how to plug it up."

VISIT FROM AUSTRALIA

A LITTLE MORE THAN a week ago, my sister, Margarete, and brother-in-law, Tony, came from Australia to visit us for three weeks.

Tony showed a great interest into our wild animals—how a woodchuck or skunk looks, and so forth. At night, we regularly have animals in our yard, so I told him I could show him.

I catch the animals regularly to take them out of the yard. I take them all to the reservation in the woods. So I put out big traps up for the woodchucks, and I got one. Tony and my sister took a look, and he said, "Hey, this is not a bad-looking animal—kind of fat."

We took it to the reservation, where I let it go.

I caught the skunk a day later in a different trap. The traps for the skunk have to be smaller, so it cannot swing up and spray, and as long it cannot spray it doesn't smell. Tony looked again and said, "Nice, but it doesn't smell. How come?"

I told him, "You are so lucky—just wait."

After the skunk went to the reservation, Tony was still wondering how a skunk smells. I never get sprayed when I release them, so there is no smell; they're just happy to run away.

He did not have to wait too long. This night another skunk came around and must have wanted to educate him, because it stank, and how. Tony and Grete came out of their bedroom bleary-eyed the next morning, and he said, "Good grief! This smell is terrible—I could not sleep at all. It choked me!"

I told him, "That was a skunk. And they smell because they like to eat their food with onions." I started to laugh. "Now you'll be able to tell them all in Australia what they're missing. Want to see one again? It's in the trap."

"You want me to go home? There I don't have to worry about this skunk-onion smell. Our onions do smell too, but better."

We caught this skunk, and several others, while Grete and Tony were here. He eventually got used to the smell, and he even went with me to release them in the reservation.

You want to know how come I did not kill them there. Believe me, kill them, and they stink just as bad—even when they're dead. It's easier to trap them and just let them run somewhere far away in the woods; let them find a new home, hopefully not too close to somebody else.

We had also much fun watching some deer and wild turkeys in the reservation. Of course we went to Manhattan, and Atlantic City, and many other places. But I'm sure the talk in Australia about skunks was on the agenda very much too when they got home.

EPILOGUE

I N 1956, ANNA AND I, with our first-born daughter Hannelore, emigrated from Austria to the U.S.A. Tony and my sister emigrated from Austria to Australia in 1957. I visited them after eighteen years, in 1974. Then, for the next eighteen years, we did not see each other, until we met at my mother's house in Austria in 1992. After another thirteen years, in 2005, they came over here. Regretfully, we will most likely never see each other again in person. It's too far and too much trouble for us to fly such distances now—age has caught up with us. We remain in contact over the phone and internet, though.

So in fifty-five years, I have seen them only three times! This is really bad!

Siegfried Bader

MY WASHING MACHINE ACCIDENT

I WORKED AS A repairman in the laundry of Bergen Pines Hospital for seven years. I repaired a Washex/Extractor washing machine (model 48/36 FLA) there. These machines are gigantic, as big as a truck. My right hand got pulled into a belt-driven pulley. It ripped the thumb off my hand, left it hanging just by a piece of skin. All the other fingers had some cuts and crush injuries; on the rest of the hand, the skin was peeled half off. Laundry workers wrapped a sheet around my hand, and I walked to the emergency room of Bergen Pines Hospital. There I was treated as an emergency case and then sent by ambulance to Hackensack Medical Center.

There, Dr. Mark A. Gurland reattached the thumb to my hand by running a long pin through my thumb into my hand (the pin remained there for about five months) and operated on the hand for over six hours to sew it up. He had to use some skin for a transplant from my wrist to cover the thumb with new skin.

A week later, still in the hospital, I had a sudden respiratory arrest. I could not inhale anymore. My chest did not work—it was paralyzed. If my wife had not been visiting me at that moment, I would not be here today. I was not able to push the emergency button anymore before passing out.

It took an hour and fifteen minutes for the emergency crews to revive me and get me to breathe again. Dr. Vaidya did a full medical checkup of my body to find the cause of that respiratory arrest, but no good explanation ever emerged.

I was discharged on May 14, 1987, but I had to go back on May 25 for a partial amputation of my thumb. Part of it had not made it, and more repairs were needed on the hand. This operation three and a half hours while I was awake, because of the possibility of another respiratory arrest; I only had local anesthesia to the arm. Dr. Vaidya had still no diagnosis about the respiratory arrest and ordered more tests, all of which were inconclusive.

From June 1987 to January 1988 I had to go two to three times a week to the Valley Hospital, in Ridgewood, for therapy to my hand. At the same time, I saw Dr. Gurland at regular intervals.

November 9, 1987, was my first day back to work after seven month of recuperation from the accident. Dr. Gurland had not been at all sure at the beginning if I would ever be able to use my hand again. But with much therapy, and exercising myself for hours at home, I found I could again perform all repairs on the machines in the laundry.

On February 1, 1993, I retired from Bergen Pines.

WHAT AGE AM I NOW?

TODAY IS MY BIRTHDAY; now I'm a year older. Yesterday I was eighty-one—or did I write eighteen? At this age, I'm getting a little dyslexic. There is the question does the "one" go before or after the "eight" if I write it out as a numeral. Today I'm twenty-eight—or is it eighty-two? What does it matter? You say there is a difference, of either one year from eighty-one to eighty-two or of ten from eighteen to twenty-eight. There we go again: Ten or one—is the zero in front of the one or behind?

So what? They're only numbers. I'm just as old as I feel. You want to know? I don't want to disappoint you or make you confused, or you might get this dyslexia, too. I'm feeling like sixty-six today; this way, I can enjoy my retirement and not feel, every Monday, Oh, I have to go to work again—and so far away from weekend relaxation.

Sixty-six is about right. Try to switch this number around, and you're free from a boss at work (though not from the bossing of your spouse, believe me), but not so old you have to use a walking stick. And if you don't want to go where your wife tries to get you to go, you can claim,

"Too far, too tired. Just go shopping by yourself" (This makes her happy, too: I'm not there to ask her, "Do we need this, really?"). There is a lot more stuff to twizzle out at sixty-six, but you have to find your own way. I cannot tell you; otherwise, my wife will learn too much about the scheme, and I'll lose my control.

I have to stop writing—my wife is coming, I cannot let her read this, or I'll get a kick in my pants, you know.

WHEN A WOMAN
CLEANS THE HOUSE

AS MOST MEN KNOW, when a woman cleans the house is time to disappear in a faraway place where he is not in her way anymore.

Today is Wednesday, the day before Thanksgiving, and my wife is busy cleaning for tomorrow. She says, "You are in my way," and points to where she wants me to go instead. Once I'm there, she says, "Hey, I have to vacuum here. I have to clean here. Go somewhere else." Then comes, "Now, what are you doing here? I just cleaned here, and you've messed it up again." A minute later: "Move! I have no time to sneak around behind you! I'm in a hurry."

By then, I'd been pushed around enough. "What is this? I live here, too. This is my house, too! After all I'm the man Of the house, am I not?"I went on with some more gremlins just so she would understand that I'm not a pushover.

"Just be quiet and stop talking," she finally said. Ha! thought I. Now I should, not only make room for her, but stop talking, too? So I proceeded to the middle of the room and shouted, "Kikerikeeee, kikerikeeee!"

"What's that supposed to mean?" she asked.

"I'm not allowed to talk, so I'm trying to sound like a rooster instead—after all, I am the rooster here."

This did not go over so well. "And I'm the hen, and this is my nest."

With that, she stopped in front of me, looking just like a hen, arms outstretched, hair standing straight up, ready to give it to me with the broom in her hand that she was swinging.

I'd better retreat, I concluded. I ran into the toilet and locked the door. In the mood she was in, maybe I would be a cooked rooster on the dining table tomorrow.

After a while, there was a knock on the door. "Open up," she said.

I am not dumb, but where to hide in the bathroom if she broke the door down? In the bathtub, with the shower doors closed? Or in the toilet? Too small; I don't fit in it. Definitely not; so I opened the door, and my wife was standing there with a can of soda. Handing it to me, she said, "You were in there too long. I didn't want you to be thirsty."

I guess my imitation of a rooster must have made an impression on her—or could it be that I'm the Beloved Husband after all?

WHEN YOU GET OLDER,
YOU SLOW DOWN!

AT TIMES WHEN I'M not busy, I think back when I was young, and how athletic and fast I was. Now I that I've really slowed down, I'm assuming (I regret I never tried it) that it would be hard for me to climb the stairs of the Empire State Building in less than half an hour.

Oh, yes—I was really athletic once. For example, I liked to play baseball, but I was the only kid in the neighborhood, so I had to play by myself. I put up the bases and the pitcher's mound, then stepped up to the mound and threw the ball as fast as I could, just like a pitcher. Then I ran fast—and I mean fast—to home plate, grabbed the bat, and batted the ball as it reached me. Then I ran to catch the ball; if I got it, this was an out for me, of course. . .but sometimes I missed the ball. Then I had to pick it up and run to first base to tag myself out. This was a little harder I could run unbelievably fast then. (Can you believe it?)

I liked to ride with my bicycle too, especially going up a mountain. No road was too steep; I tackled them all. You should have seen the faces of the automobile drivers when I passed them up on these steep hills; the cars were laboring and just barely made it; it was very amusing for me.

One day I was pedaling on a particularly steep hill, going downhill. I was rolling so fast that the wind I created when I passed hikers blew their hats off their heads! But I had a little problem: When I tried to brake because I was going too fast, the brake stopped working. This was not that much of a problem, though. Remember how fast I could run? I just jumped off my bike, turned around, running backwards in front of the bike, grabbed the handle bars, and slowed the bike to the speed I wanted. I mounted the bike again, though from time to time I had to repeat this when the bike started moving too fast, until I got home and fixed the brakes.

One time when I drove up the mountain with my bike, I encountered a broken-down car, with two men in it, parked on the side of the road. There were no cell-phones at the time, so they didn't know how to get help. I told them I'd help them. My first idea was to lift the front of the bike up, put the front wheel in the trunk of the car, and push them up. Then I realized there were three of us, and we had all a belt to hold our pants up, so I tied the belts together, secured one end on the front bumper, the other end to the basket of my bike, and off we went. It was hard peddling my bike up the hill with the car, but I did made it all the way up. When I had them on the top of the hill, I gave them their belts back and put mine into my pants. We were so glad we could get our belts back, because by then our pants were around our ankles. Luckily, my underwear was clean.

I gained another good thing from all of this. The basket on the bike got stretched to twice its size from pulling that car; now I could put twice as much into it. And what did the car do? When it started to roll down the other side of the hill, it just started—and they drove off without a "thank you."

Every time I ran into a problem, I could always solve it—the way I did when I was driving to Canada to pick up my wife since she was visiting her brother (no, not with my bike, of course). After driving for many hours, it was late in the afternoon, and I stopped at a little diner for something to eat. They had, for their daily special, beans. There were baked beans, bean salad, and navy bean soup—well you get the idea.

Luckily, I love beans. So I stuffed myself with all kinds of beans. I really liked them all. By the time I left that diner, night had fallen, and I had driven on for an hour when I realized I needed gas for the car, but I couldn't find a station that was still open. So I kept going till the car stopped in the middle of nowhere.

So now what? I wondered. Where will I get gas? This was the only one time in my life I was totally lost; I did not know what to do.

Then I got help from an unexpected source. My belly started to grumble. Oh, the beans. . . .

Beans, of course, produce gas, and, after all those

beans, I had plenty of gas. It was a little awkward to get it into the tank, but I managed. Thanks to the beans, I made it to the next town—and just before I ran out of this bean-gas, I found an open gas station and filled the tank with gasoline.

Now that I'm old ("old" sounds so, so depressing; let's say "a little older"—I feel better already!), I don't walk as much as I did when I was younger. I loved to walk, whether it was in the mountains or along a river. I especially liked to walk into the woods, which was always so soothing—listening to birds sing, then looking up into the trees to locate them and guessing what kinds of birds they were.

I was not that good at identifying what species of birds they were; the most I know about birds is that they have feathers. If the creature had feathers, it was a bird. If the creature had hair, it was a squirrel, period, even if it was as big as a dog. I know I should try to identify them all better, but I walked to exercise my lungs and legs, not my gray matter. That was something for my wife to do if she was walking with me. She knows the trees and birds and everything else. Most of the time I walked alone, because, when it came to long-distance walking in the woods, my wife always for some reason had something else to do.

Let me tell you of a walk into the woods when I discovered a third type of creature. That day I walked for quite a distance into the woods, and it disturbed me when I suddenly felt nature calling and it was not number one.

What to do? I sure couldn't wait until I got home. What the heck, I told myself—I'm alone, and there are plenty of bushes around, so I made use of the facilities.

But I had no toilet paper. What will I do now? I wondered. Use my handkerchief? Oh, no! I could not do that! I would not be able to blow my nose in any handkerchief again.

I looked around and noticed that there was something growing on a vine, but the leaves were too small. Afterward, I discovered that this was poison ivy (was I glad I hadn't used it!). Then there were some larger leafy plants. I figured those leaves were better.

What in my haste I did not see was that they were full of ants, and I discovered the third type of creature right after I pulled my pants up. If somebody had seen the dance I performed then without music. . . .

From that day on, I know what they mean when they say, "Do you have ants in your pants?" Just try it—you'll never forget why.

If you don't believe some of these stories, you *can* believe that I like to ice-skate, too. No matter how large the lake was, as long it was frozen I ice-skated around it. But one day the ice was a little thinner, and I was not sure—should I or should I not ice-skate? But the winter was almost over, and in the summer there is no ice.

This was a mistake. In the middle of the lake, the ice gave away, and I was quickly sank into the water. I wondered what to do, and I told myself, "You are so athletic—

do something!" So I reached behind me, grabbed my shirt by the collar, pulled myself out, dragged myself off the ice to the shore, and cried out as loudly as I could, "SOS, SOS!" It was all I ever heard when there was an emergency on the radio shows then. What it meant, I didn't know. Probably that you were in some kind of a big sauce, the same thing as yelling 911. Remember, we did not have cell phones then—but"SOS" was just as good. They came and revived me, and they told me I was so lucky that I was strong enough to pull myself out like that.

Just think, if I hadn't been there, nobody else would have rescued me, and I would not have been able to write all this now.

What you read on the first and second pages is all of course utterly honest and truthful!

I guarantee that.

www.ingramcontent.com/pod-product-compliance
Lightning Source LLC
Chambersburg PA
CBHW030821090426
42737CB00009B/816